The False Prophet, Alias Another Beast

A Volume of the Eschatology Series

Donald Peart

*The False Prophet, Alias, Another Beast Copyright © 1997
Donald A. Peart*

All rights reserved. No part of this book may be reproduced in any form, except for the inclusion of brief quotations in a review, without permission in writing from the author or publisher.

ISBN: 0-9702301-0-9

- *The New King James is the Bible translation used, unless otherwise noted*
- *All bold text and literal parenthetical phrases in the Scripture references are added by the author for clarity*
- *Dictionary reference, includes, but not limited to, Strong's Concordance, BibleWorks Software, and ISA2 Basic Software*

Cover design by Donald Peart Jr.

Acknowledgments

In sincere appreciation I credit the Holy Spirit who provided the revelation which is set forth in this book. I also acknowledge two men of God, among many, who have imparted to me important concepts acknowledged in this book, Dr. Kelley Varner of Richland North Carolina, and Dr. Joshua (Turnel) Nelson of Trinidad & Tobago, both of whom are now with the Lord Jesus.

Table of Contents

Preface
Introduction----------------------------------1

Mystery Unveiled--------------------------3
Wolves in Sheep's Clothing
Unlawful Alliance
Deceitful Doctrines
Shaken Minds; Shaken Faith
The Divorce from God
Lawless Energy
The False Prophet(s)
The Restrainer of the Lawless one
Let the Anointing of God Keep You
Initiation by Blood
Deceiver of Nations
The Coming Lamb (Jesus)
Foxes that Spoil the Fruit

Dominion in the Unseen------------------23
King Angels
Satan, the Prince of satans
Rulers of This Dark Age
Controlling Spirits
Created to Help; Fell to Cause Adversity
Violent Rain
Geshem, the Enemy
Be You Separated Unto God
Wandering Stars
Seduction
Wrong Influence
The Friendship of the World

Man or Beast------------------------------45
Dressed Like a Sheep
Mutation
Angelic Beasts
Mankind Marrying Angels
Men with the Hearts of Beasts
The False Prophet, the Man
The spirit of error
The spirit of python
Aliases

The Spirit Giver----------------------------59
The Father of Lies
Traveler or Wanderer?
The Lie-Homoerotic
Cause and Effect
Reanimation
Mystery of Iniquity Revitalized
Self Worship
Wrong Photocopy
Fame
The Dumb Idol That Spoke
Marked to Perdition (666)

The False Prophet's Demise--------------77
Sovereign Lord
Set Time (42 Months)
Rulers of Darkness Bound to God's Time
God's Royal Edict - It's Law
God's Region of Fire
Death by Fire

Preface

Greetings to you in the name of our Lord Jesus Christ! The Spirit of the Lord has directed me to write this first volume of three. He said, "Send it to the seven Churches, sown across the land." The Lord instructed me to prophesy against the false prophet, and <u>cast</u> him <u>down.</u> I am to speak **to** his (the false prophet's) purposes, and prophesy his demise.

I have, therefore, set forth in order this synoptic book. The book is brief for many reasons. One of the reasons is that most of the youth of today do not have the patience to read extensive writings. Therefore, this is catering to their need that they might have an understanding about the times to come. However, for the person who enjoys serious study, there are many references. These references will assist the serious student. The references will also broaden his or her understanding.

It is also my desire that all readers read the entire book for an accurate understanding of the book. This is because some of the teachings of this book were hidden from other generations. However, the Spirit is now revealing these mysteries to his apostles and prophets. The book also explains itself as you read each chapter. I pray each chapter may be enlightening to you, strengthening your resistance against the spirit of false prophets, by the anointing in you.

Blessings,
Donald Peart, called to be a son of God

Chapter 1
Introduction

Are there false prophets among us today? The answer to this question is yes. In every generation, there seems to be a quest to seek prophetic knowledge. This hunger in humanity is the gateway by which false prophets present themselves to be accepted. The **blind** pursuit of prophetic understanding is what causes people not to see the true nature of false prophets. As a result, the false ones are accepted as speaking the truth.

Thus, this sincere hunger can be filled with all the illusions of the prophet of darkness. Or should I say the illusions of the **spirits of error** in the false prophets. This is significant because these snakes (spirits of error) can detect this hunger.

One should conclude that the Church and the world should be taught how to recognize the spirits behind false prophets. Once this is accomplished, the false prophets can no longer deceive so easily. There is a spirit behind every false prophet (See I John 4). This hints to us that falsehood is demonstrated by the inward nature of the deceivers. Or, false prophets can be known by the fruit they produce.

Spirits have the ability to bear fruits. The **Holy Spirit** produces all good fruit (Gal. 5: 22-23). Our Lord Jesus, who is blessed forevermore, emphatically taught that we should recognize false prophets by the fruits they bear. Similarly, Jesus' true prophets are known by **the fruit of the Holy Spirit.**

True prophets are full of good fruits, without partiality, bringing to light all that is false. Jesus always warns of deceptions to come. Therefore, the Lord does not want any in His Church to be deceived. As Ezra and his colleagues **distinctly** gave the **sense** of the law of God, so likewise, God's prophets shall give a **precise** understanding of the writing of truth.

This is done as the Lord is inviting **all** to draw near to him, in order for **all** to see the fruit of the Spirit clearly. The purpose is to empower the Church to recognize the corrupt fruit of the false prophets. With this in mind, I now conclude this introduction by telling of an event.

My family and I were driving to Jacksonville, North Carolina, from Baltimore, Maryland. During the trip, I saw a banana plant (so I thought). I got excited. It reminded me of when I was a child growing up in the West Indies. Banana plants are common along some roadsides. I said to my wife and children, in the Jamaican vernacular, "Look, a 'banana tree'!" My wife and children got excited, ready to see what a "banana plant" looks like.

The closer I got to the plant, the more I realized it might not be a banana plant. So, I proceeded to look for the **flower** of the fruit, or **the banana fruit** itself. I saw none. However, the plant looked so close to a real Banana plant; I said to myself, "It must be a real banana plant."

However, the closer I came to the plant the more I realized it was not a banana plant. First, there was no **flower** for the fruit. Secondarily, there was **no fruit**. Finally, the plant **looked like** a banana plant, but, in reality, it was not. I conclude with Jesus' statement concerning the false prophets, **"Ye [you] shall know them by their fruits"** (Matt. 7:16).

Chapter 2
Mystery Unveiled

2 Thess 2:7, KJV:
*For the mystery of iniquity doth already work: only he who now letteth [withhold] will let [withhold], **until he be taken out of the way**.*

Ever since the days of old, the people of God have encountered false prophets. Jeremiah, Ezekiel, Paul, and John the Beloved, had many confrontations with false prophets. Jesus says, "And many false prophets shall arise, and shall deceive many" (Matt. 24:11).

The false prophet himself is **one** of the mysteries in the book of Revelation. This mystery will be explicated in this volume. The purposes of the false prophet need to be spoken **of** because of the critical role he plays in deceiving the world. For some, this will result in the acceptance of the first beast, whose name is blasphemy (Rev. 13:1).

First, I will begin the study with views from other books. These views include: the unveiling of false prophets by the Lord, along with his apostles and prophets. One will also learn the power, and spirit(s), behind the false prophets, including their deceitful doctrines. The chapter will then conclude with a brief look at the foxes that spoil the fruits.

Wolves in Sheep's Clothing

Matt. 7:15-16, KJV:
[15]Beware of false prophets, which come to you in sheep's clothing, but inwardly they are ravening wolves. [16]Ye shall know them by their fruits. Do men gather grapes of thorns, or figs of thistles?

The first understanding a person can receive from Jesus' statements is that in order to locate a false prophet, one must be able to see inwardly. This is because Jesus says, "**inwardly** they are ravening wolves." The Holy Spirit shed some light on this truth in John's epistles.

1 John 4:1-3, KJV:
*¹Beloved, believe not every spirit, but try the spirits whether they are of God: because many false prophets are gone out into the world. ²Hereby know ye the Spirit of God: Every **spirit that confesseth** that Jesus Christ is come in the flesh is of God: ³And every spirit that confesseth not that Jesus Christ is come in the flesh is not of God: and this is that spirit of the antichrist, whereof ye heard that it should come; and even now already is it in the world.*

John made it plain that the only way to identify false prophets is by **knowing the spirits** of the prophets. A person must have the ability to see what the prophet's **spirit is confessing, not necessarily his mouth.** A prophet confessing with his mouth should not convince a person that he is speaking the truth. On the contrary, the **prophet's spirit** must also agree with what his mouth is saying. His spirit must confess that Jesus is come in the flesh (John 1:14; 1 Cor. 6:19).

Jesus taught that a person knows falsehood by inward fruits. John also taught that a person knows the prophets by the invisible part of a man, **the spirit.** Christians must open their eyes to see by the Spirit (Luke 10:23-24; 1 Cor. 12:10). This will enable them to see the falsehood. Again, I emphasize that for any prophet to be true, **his spirit must say the same thing his mouth is saying**.

This is why it is important to live the life of Jesus inwardly and not just outwardly in form or fashion. Many false prophets shall arise, and deceive many. They will appear righteous outwardly; but inwardly they are wolves. These false prophets do not have the gentleness of Christ, but a vicious beastly nature. They have an **unlawful** alliance with **the beasts of the field.**

Unlawful Alliance

Ezek. 22:25, KJV:
*There is a **conspiracy (lit., unlawful alliance) of** her prophets in the midst thereof, like roaring lions ravening the prey; they have devoured souls; they have taken the treasures and precious things; they have made her widows in the midst thereof.*

Matt. 7:21-23, KJV:
*21Not every one that saith unto me, Lord, Lord, shall enter into the kingdom of heaven; but he that doeth the will of the Father which is in heaven. 22Many will say to me in that day Lord, Lord, have we not prophesied in thy name? and in thy name cast out devils? and in thy name done many wonderful works? 23And then will I profess unto them, I never knew you: depart from me, **ye that work iniquity.***

The spirits of these prophets confess beastliness. They are allied with lawlessness; and they work lawlessness. Our Lord declares this plainly when he says false prophets are **"workers** of iniquity" (Matt. 7:23). In the Greek, the phrase literally says, "you that **work lawlessness." (The author supplies all emphasis in this book).** Jesus says, "They are working lawlessness." The false prophets **thought** they did many wonderful works (lit., works of power) in Jesus' name.

In other words, the false prophets thought they were doing works through Jesus. But, in reality, they were doing works by a lawless power. Do you see it? These false prophets are working (showing signs and wonders) by an **unlawful alliance with beasts.** This is sad, because some of them do not know it. The apostle Paul also dealt with other aspects of this deceitful work of lawlessness. This is seen in his second letter to the Thessalonians.

Deceitful Doctrines

2 Thess. 2:3, KJV:
Let no man deceive *you by any means: for that day shall not come, except there come a falling away first, and that man of sin be revealed, the son of perdition:*

In Chapter 2 of 2 Thessalonians, Paul warns them not to be soon shaken or troubled by **spirit,** words or letters, which false teachers claimed to be written by him. There were some false teachers that said the day of Christ had set in. The apostle then proceeds to tell **why** Christ's day cannot come **just yet.** Paul starts with an interesting statement in verse 3. He says, "Let no man **deceive** you by any means…."

So, if a person believes any other declaration than what Paul is about to say, **that person is deceived.** The first work of the false prophet is deception (Rev. 13:14). Paul continues, *"For that day shall not come except there come a falling away **first,** and that man of sin **(lit., lawlessness),** be revealed, the son of perdition;"* **(A. S. Worrel).**

This is saying that if anyone believes that Christ will come before the falling away and the revealing of the man of lawlessness, that person is deceived. A person might ask, "Why is this deception so important?" It is important because it causes believers to be shaken in mind and faith (compare 2 Tim. 2:18).

Shaken Minds; Shaken Faith

2 Thess. 2:2, KJV:
*That you be not soon **shaken** in mind, or be troubled, **neither by spirit,** nor by word, nor by letters as from us, as that the day of Christ is at hand.*

False teachers taught the saints of that day that the day of Christ is at hand. That is that day of Christ is occurring presently. They also thought they had missed the day of Christ. **This teaching shook them.** However, Paul told them not to be shaken, nor troubled by **spirit** (i.e., the false prophet), nor by letters. The reason is that at least two things must happen before Christ comes.

The falling away (illegal, or lawless divorce), and the man of lawlessness (the first beast of Rev. 13) must occur **first.** However, if a person is convinced that Christ must come first (before the falling away, and the man of sin's manifestation) when the seducing spirits do cause the apostasy (falling away), that person will believe the false prophets are true prophets. The Thessalonians exemplified this in that they became troubled believing the false teachers, demonstrating they were almost deceived, had Paul not addressed the false teaching!

Today we are also taught that Jesus is supposed to come first, before these kinds of events take place. Oh! Beloved this is destructive. The heart of the simple will wander. Peoples' faith will be overthrown (compare 2 Tim. 2:18). They will not have the faith to stand when the mystery beast is manifested. This false doctrine given to the Body of Christ will cause "the faith to depart from some," because of **a lack of preparation** (2 Corinthians 14:8 with Ezek. 13:1-6).

1 Tim. 4:1, KJV:
*Now the Spirit speaketh expressly, that in the latter times **some shall depart from the faith**, giving heed to seducing spirits, and doctrines of devils;*

The middle of this verse in the Interlinear Bible, Second Edition, by John P. Green, Sr. reads "will depart from1 some the faith." An understanding is that not only will some depart[1] from the faith, but through the doctrine of seducing spirits, the faith in Jesus will depart from some (contrast Rev. 14:12, KJV). This is true because all men will not retain God in their knowledge (Rom. 1:28). Please meditate on these things, and the Lord will give you understanding (2 Tim. 2:7; 2 Pet. 3:16).

It is important that Christians understand the mystery of lawlessness- for so **iniquity** means in 2 Thess. 2:1-7. False prophets will arise. They will cause many to fall away, or divorce from Christ, exemplifying the ultimate deceptions. The first deception is to believe one can live without the law of God, which is lawlessness (Ps. 2:2-3). The second deception is to believe **the lie over the truth.**

The lie is, believing the man of **sin (lit., lawlessness)** is God (2 Thess. 2). In other words, some will illegally divorce the true Christ. Anyone who believes the day of Christ will come first, before the falling away, and the man of sin being revealed, Paul calls that person deceived. In the words of Paul, "Let no man deceive **you** by any means" (2 Thess. 2:3). **Note: This topic will be developed further in the next volumes.**

The Divorce from God

There must be a falling away **first**. Some will forsake the holy covenant (Dan. 11:30-32). As the Scripture above says: "**Some shall depart from the faith, giving heed to seducing spirits**" (1 Tim. 4:1). The false prophet or antichrist is among these seducers. He shall ascend from the underworld (1 John 4:1; Rev. 13:11). He will be one of the leading angels, seducing many to fall away from the faith.

---

[1] *Greek: aposteésontaí an inflection of aphistemi, from apo (off away from something near) and histemi (to stand); hence to depart from, to stand off, etc.*

The Greek definition for the words falling away in 2 Thessalonians 2:3 is **"to divorce,"** and to revolt against a state (government, city, etc.). This truth gives light to 1 Tim. 4:1-3.

1 Tim. 4:1-3, KJV:
1 Now the Spirit speaketh expressly, that in the latter times some shall **depart (act, instigate to revolt)** *from the faith, giving heed to seducing spirits, and doctrines of devils;2 Speaking lies in hypocrisy; having their conscience seared with a hot iron;3* **Forbidding (lit, estop) to marry** ...

This doctrine of "forbidding marrying" can be looked at from many viewpoints. However, I will only look at it from one point of view. The word **forbidding** literally means **"estop"** (Strong's #2967).

"Estop" means "to prevent from asserting, or doing something contrary to previous assertion or act. This word forbidding is the same word Paul used in 1 Thessalonians 2. He used it to show how the Jews were **contrary** to all men.

1 Thess. 2:14-16, KJV:
14 For ye brethren, became followers of the Churches of God which in Judea are in Christ Jesus: for ye also have suffered like things of your own countrymen, even as they have of the Jews: 15 Who both killed the Lord Jesus, and their own prophets, and have persecuted us; and they please not God, and are **contrary** *to all men: 16* **Forbidding** *us to speak to the Gentiles that they might be saved, to fill up their sins alway: for the wrath is come upon them to the uttermost.*

The Jews were trying to stop Paul from doing something contrary to what they asserted, which was separation from the Gentiles. So likewise, the correct assertion of marriage is to remain married. However, the seducing spirits will try to prevent this assertion.

These spirits will cause marriage to go **contrary.** The phrase **"forbidding marrying"** can now be seen from a different view. The Scripture is saying that seducers will be trying to stop the marriage process from continuing on.

These spirits will cause a prevalence of divorce in the Body of Christ, a sign of the ultimate divorce to come. The ultimate divorce is a divorce from God. This divorce is significant, because as stated before, divorce is one of the definitions for the words "falling away" (2 Thess. 2:3).

"Falling away" is the Greek word apostasia, which is the feminine of apostasion. Apostasion is defined as **divorce, or a writing of divorcement** (Matt. 5:31; Strong's # 646, # 647). The seducing spirits will attack God's person concerning his stewardship of the earth.

This will cause some Christians <u>not</u> to remain married to God. In essence, there will be a **political divorce** from the kingdom of heaven. It is political, because these saints will join another kingdom. They will renounce their heavenly citizenship, and become counselors for another state -the kingdom of the beast to come.

Dan. 11:30, KJV:
For the ships of Chittim shall come against him: therefore he shall be grieved, and return, and have indignation against the holy covenant: so shall he do; he shall even return and have **intelligence** *with them that* **forsake** *the holy covenant.*

The man of sin will "have indignation against the holy covenant" — the new covenant saints (Rev. 13:6-7). He will return, and have intelligence (counseling) with them that **forsake** the holy covenant. However, those who remain alive until the coming of the Lord must be strong against these divorces

(Hebrews 10:38-39; Dan. 11:32). For the beast will cause them to disassociate from the sanctified.

Dan. 11:32, KJV:
And such as do wickedly against the covenant shall he corrupt by **flatteries:** *but the people that know their God shall be strong, and do exploits.*

The first segment of this prophecy can also read, "And such as do wickedly against the holy covenant shall **be caused to dissemble**" (see margin Thompson Chain Reference Bible, Fifth Improved Edition, emphasis mine). But the people who **know** their God will be strong (against these hypocrites and the beast) and will do exploits.

These **antichrists** will disguise their real plan and nature behind a mask (1John 2:18). Their plan is to stealthily cause more divorce from God in the Church (1 Pet. 2:1-2). They will **pretend** to be walking in the true Spirit of God while they knowingly walk in the power, or **energy** of Satan.

Lawless Energy[2]

2 Thess. 2:11, KJV:
And for this cause God shall send them **strong** *delusion, that they should believe* **a lie (lit.,, the lie).**

The word **"strong"** literally means energy — Greek, energeia. **Energia** is the compound of two words: en (in) and ergon (work, toil). These are the words from which we get our English word en-ergy. Therefore, energy means to work-in.

---

[2] *The use of the word "energy" is in no way associated with the New Age doctrine. In fact, they are perverting its' use as the reader will see in this book.*

There is a lawless **energy (the capacity to do work)** going across the land, causing the world, and some saints, to separate from and distrust the only true God. This is the **illegal "energy"** the New Age movement is following. Jesus revealed that this is the kind of sin the Holy Spirit will convict the world of. They believe not on Jesus, but in something or someone else (John 16:7-8).

False prophets will preach the lie that God will come in the form of the first beast (2 Thess. 2; Rev. 13). They will also work the lawless power of the devil. They will do this by sending the energy (in-working) of delusion to convince the **earth** and them that **dwell on the earth** that they are indeed true prophets (2 Thess. 2:9-10; I John 4:1; Rev. 13:12). Most people of the earth will believe the false power. **This means** they will believe the power of Satan is the power of God (2 Cor. 11:14). In turn they will divorce God and **"kiss"** the beast in **remarriage.**

Rev. 13:4, KJV:
*And they worshipped the dragon which gave power unto the beast: and they **worshipped (lit., kissed)** the beast, saying, who is like unto the beast? who is able to make war with him?*

The people of the earth **kissed the beast in marriage**. One of the reasons is that the false prophet proclaimed that the beast was the ultimate **war** machine to come (Dan. 7:19; Rev. 13:4; Rev. 13:12, 14-15). They show their loyalty by saying, "who is like unto the beast?" Yet, the question is, "how does this one beast deceive the world?" First, one must remember he is not alone.

The False Prophet(s)

There will be seducing spirits (plural) (1 Tim. 4:1; Rev. 16:13). Most importantly, spirits can transform themselves from one being into many **mouths.** They can **work-in** a person who will allow them to (Rev. 16:13; 2 Chronicles 18).

In the days of Ahab and Jehoshaphat, four hundred prophets prophesied to these two kings. The Scripture teaches that **one** lying spirit **multiplied** himself in the **mouth of** these **four hundred** false prophets. Spirits have the ability to **reproduce** themselves <u>out of one being into a current of air</u> (Strong's # 4151, Rev. 16:13).

One spirit is then able **to cover, and work-in** the mouth of a multitude of prophets (2 Chronicles 18; contrast 1 Sam. 9:7-13). The false prophet is also an **earthly** spirit who can expand himself to cover a multitude of prophets (James 3:15; Rev. 13:11; Rev. 16:13). He can thus promulgate (spread) his deception at large. As a matter of fact, he is now preparing the minds of the people of the earth, and some in the Church, to receive him. He is doing this by the illegal, and counterfeit, "energeia" of Satan (2 Thess. 2:9). Notice, I said, "energeia" [energy], which stimulates feelings and thoughts **within.** How?

Remember energy literally means, to work-**in.** It is the fake **in-working** that produces false signs and wonders in false religions (compare Rev. 16:13-14; and **2 Thess. 2:9**). In 2 Thess. 2:9, NIV, part of the verse reads, "the **work** of Satan displayed in all kinds of counterfeit miracles, signs and wonders." This literally reads, "'**energeia**' [in-work] of Satan...."

Paul, in this text, states that Satan has the capacity to do work in wardly. However, for the beloved saints, greater is He [Jesus] who is in you than any force in the world (see 1 John 4:4). Satan's work, though, is illegal, fake, and deceptive. The whole purpose of the deception is to cause the falling away from God. The false prophet's (one of the Satans) intention is significant because the man of lawlessness cannot be revealed **until** the falling away comes **first** (2 Thess. 2:8).

The Restrainer of the Lawless one

2 Thess. 2:7, KJV:
For the mystery of iniquity doth already work: only he who now **letteth** *[Old Eng., to delay] will* **let [to delay]**, *until he be taken out of the way.*

The falling away is a sign that the lawless power of the devil is in full force. It is the indication that the man of sin is about to be revealed. Part of the restrainer that is holding back, or delaying the man of lawlessness is the falling away, or divorce from God. Paul told the Thessalonians about the man of sin coming. However, he did not tell them what is delaying the man of sin from **coming into being**.

He says, "5Remember ye not when I was yet with you, I told you these things? **6And now you know what withholdeth** that he might be revealed in his time" (2 Thess. 2:5-6). Paul says, "Now you know what witholdeth …." How did they know? He had just told them in verse 3 "what" is restraining the man of sin. The falling away must come first (compare Rev. 12:4).

Paul goes on to explain it more by saying, "For the mystery of iniquity (lit., lawlessness) doth already work: only he who now letteth **(lit., only the restrainer)** will let **(lit., will restrain)**, until he (the beast) be taken out of the way **(or until he be birthed out of the middle)**." One indication of the restrainer being in place is the falling away not occurring, as yet. According to Paul the apostasy must take place, first. This is the same as saying the restrainer must be removed, first.

The mystery of lawlessness — antichrist spirit — is already working (1 John 4:3). But, the beast cannot manifest himself until the ultimate deception is finished. The deception is the spirit of the false prophet [working through his lying prophets (I John 4) causing some from the holy nation to transgress against the New Covenant. Once the apostasy is accomplished, the man of sin will come on the scene. He will not work mysteriously anymore. This can be seen more clearly in the book of Daniel.

In the book of Daniel, the prophet gives some exposition on the falling away. He used terms like, "them that forsake the holy covenant;" and "transgression against the daily sacrifice" to describe the divorce from God. Daniel speaks of a little horn (the beast) that became very great. "Yea, he magnified himself even **to (lit., against)** the **Prince of Host [Jesus]**" (Dan. 8:11). In his discourse Daniel goes on to say why this horn was allowed to do what he did.

Dan. 8:12, KJV:
*And an host was given him against the daily sacrifice **by reason of transgression,** and it cast down the truth to the ground; and it practiced, and prospered.*

The first section of the verse alternately reads, "A host was given over to him **for the transgression against the daily sacrifice**" (Thompson Chain Reference, Fifth Improved Edition). The Interlinear Bible says, "And a host was given with the daily sacrifice **because of transgression ...**" The reading in the original context makes the difference.

The true meaning is hinted in the King James Version but it is not very clear. Nevertheless, these other texts make it plain. The reason why the host is given over to the "little horn" is because the host transgressed **(lit., revolt, apostasy)** against the daily (or perpetual) sacrifice **[Jesus]**. Daniel did not quite understand the message and sought the meaning for clarification (Dan. 8:15-16). Then the angel gave the interpretation.

Dan. 8:23, KJV:
And in the latter time of their kingdom, ***when transgressors are come to the full,*** *a king of fierce countenance, and understanding dark sentences shall stand up.*

We understand from this passage that the transgressors (lit., revolters) must come to "the full." "When the transgressors are come to the **full,**" **then** will the king **stand up!** Daniel bears witness to the fact that the "full" falling away must come **first.** I want to reiterate reluctantly that some will forsake the holy covenant to fulfill the fullness of transgressions.

Then will the scarlet colored beast ascend from the bottomless pit. False prophets will arise and seduce many. This will occur before the man of sin arises, and before our Lord Jesus comes. And, when Jesus comes, He will destroy the beast with the spirit of his mouth and the brightness of his coming. Jesus shall be revealed from heaven in flames of fire (1 Thess. 1:7; 2 Thess. 2:8; Rev. 19:20-21).

Let the Anointing of God Keep You

Therefore, allow the true anointing of the Lord Jesus to keep you. Do not be deceived into believing "the lie." The mystery of lawlessness does exist. The spirit of the false prophet **is already in the world** (1 John 4:3). In other words, the strong delusion of Satan is already working. This is only true in those who do not retain the love of the truth (2 Thess. 2:10-11). This false **"energeia"** (anointing) is sent to cause **cheating** (the definition for the word "deceivableness" in 2 Thess. 2:10) in those who hate the truth. Thus they will be lost, unless they repent (2 Thess. 2:12).

The false prophet's **in-working** is the false anointing that is trying to work its way **in** the believer. The goal is to **influence** a person into believing the lie over the truth (contrast John 4:4). The false witness can deceive a person because he is trying to work on the inside.

Thus, one might believe the witness is God, when in fact it is not. **"But** ye [you] have an **unction (lit, anointing)** from the **Holy one**, and ye [you] know all things" (1 John 2:20). Let **that** anointing (See 1 John 2:20; 2:27) therefore **abide in you,** which you have heard from the beginning (1 John 2:24).

"These things have I written unto you concerning them that **seduce you"** (1 John 2:26). Seducers are in the land, and are working purposely by three: the dragon, the beast, and the false prophet (Rev. 16:13). Their purpose is to initiate as many as they can in their illegal practices.

Initiation by Blood

Let us look further at the word **mystery** for a better understanding of the lawless power. The word mystery means, "That which is known by the initiated." It is a secret known by the initiated. Therefore, the public at large does not know it is in operation. But the Lord who knows all things reveals these things to His people, to keep them safe.

He can thus keep His people **ahead** of the fallen ones. The Spirit revealed these mysteries to Paul, Peter, and John, just to name a few. In our day God is also revealing the Scripture to His servants. They also will **expose** the secret workings of lawlessness. The Church will then know and **resist** the mystery of lawlessness.

In every age there are false ones who are initiated into this power of lawlessness. Those initiated know the secret working of lawlessness, and are purposely walking in this power. The false prophet has some prophets, alias soothsayers, who are initiated into this mystery by blood (Isaiah 57:3-9; also see the Septuagint). Their ultimate purpose is to cause deception and revolt against the policies of heaven. They will do this with powers, signs, and lying wonders, in the nations (Rev. 20:3; Rev 18:23; Rev. 11:18).

Deceiver of Nations

The false prophet will exercise all the authority of the man of sin, which Satan gave unto the first beast (Rev. 13:12). In 2 Thess. 2:9, Paul explains that Satan will use his workings to produce **all power** (not some power), sign, and lying wonders (lit., wonders of falsehood). It is the false prophet, alias "another beast," who will exercise all the powers of lawlessness available to him. He will deceive those whose names are not written in the Book of Life.

The false prophet has targeted America as the next nation to deceive fully. The seed of deception started in the 1800's. It is now multiplying in the nation at large. Do not forget Satan is out to deceive whole nations, not just a few people (Rev. 20).

If any person wants to know the angel over America, he is called the false prophet, alias, another beast. His goal is to turn the heart of the great eagle from God unto Satan. Why? I believe it is because of perversity, ranging from tolerance of false religions, including every form of witchcraft; abuse of the poor in many ways (i.e. wages); to sexual immorality. (Malachi 3:5, NIV; 2 Thess. 2:10). Yet this can be curtailed by prayer and fasting. The Church should do this.

Look at the youth of today. If they are not following Islam, they are sacrificing their children to Satan ... literally or somewhere in the middle. I would say this is deception demonstrated. Remember, the Scripture says, the three must deceive nations: Satan, the beast, and false prophet.

Nations shall be gathered "to the battle of that great day of God Almighty" (Rev. 16:14). The Church must hold to her nation's heavenly citizenship, and be not deceived (Phil. 3:20, NIV; 1 Pet. 2:9, NIV). Soon, our Savior will descend from heaven after He manifest Himself through His Church (Jude 1:14; Rev. 22:20, NIV).

The Coming Lamb (Jesus)

Rev. 19:19, KJV:
And I saw the beast, and the kings of the earth and their armies, gathered together to make war against him that sat on the horse, and against his army.

It is at this war that the King of kings and Lord of lords will come in power and great glory, **not before.** This is why Paul says the day of Christ is **not** just at hand. In other words, Christ is not going to come in any minute. Paul also says the Christians will know the **times** (plural), and the **seasons** (plural) (2 Thess. 5:1-3).

He then explained some aspects of these times, and seasons in 2 Thess. 2. He says, "For that day shall not come, **except** there come a falling away **first, and** the man of sin be revealed, the son of perdition." The man of sin, the son of perdition, and the first beast are all the same person.

It is this beast that will gather the nations to war against **the Lamb of God.** It is **during** this gathering for war the Lord says, "Behold I come as a thief" (Rev. 16:15). **His coming is not before the war; and** no man, nor angel, knows the exact time.

Rev. 16:13-15, KJV:
13And I saw three unclean spirits like frogs come out of the mouth of the dragon, and out of the mouth of the beast, and out of the mouth of the false prophet. 14For they are spirits of devils, working miracles, which go

forth unto the kings of the earth and of the whole world, to gather them to the battle of that great day of God Almighty. ¹⁵Behold I come as a thief. Blessed is he that watcheth, and keepeth his garments, lest he walk naked, and they see his shame.

As one can see, in the midst of the gathering kings, Jesus says, "Behold I come as a thief." These verses, coupled with 2 Thess. 2:3, 1 Thess. 5, and 2 Pet. 3 are <u>some</u> of the keys to understanding the controversy that surrounds Christ's coming. I ask you a question. Do you know the **sign (singular) of Christ's coming?**

All believers should know the sign of Jesus' coming. I must admit, the mystery of His coming is "hard to be understood, which they [false prophets] that are unlearned and unstable wrest **(lit., twist)** as they do also the **other scriptures,** unto their own destruction" (2 Pet. 3:16 with 2 Pet. 2:1).

Therefore, it is given to God's apostles, prophets, evangelists, pastors, and teachers—together with the Holy Spirit—to mature the saints. We must prepare the saints to stand in that day (Eph. 4:11-14; Ezek. 13:5; I Cor. 13:8). **Please do not allow the ministry gifts of the Lord to be like Nicodemus (John 3:10).**

The Church must, and will, be mature enough not to be tossed to and fro with false miracles, and doctrines of devils (Rev. 16:13-14; 2 Thess. 2:9; 1 Tim. 4:1; Eph. 4:14). The spirit of the Lord calls **foxes** all who do not cause his people to stand in the battle.

Foxes that Spoil the Fruit

Ezek. 13:4-5, KJV:
*⁴O Israel, thy prophets are like **foxes** in the deserts. ⁵Ye have not gone up into the **gaps,** neither made up the hedges for the house of Israel to **stand** in the battle in the day of the LORD.*

While in prayer, I heard in my mind, "It is the foxes who spoil the fruits" (compare S.S. 2:15). One might ask, "What fruits?" — the fruit of going **"up into the gaps"** (i.e., prayer for another)! Standing in the gap, by prayer, is love. Moses demonstrated this (Ps. 106:19-23, KJV; Ex. 32:30-33). The false prophets, in Ezekiel's time, were not looking out for the people by prayer.

Ezekiel calls these false prophets "foxes." It is these foxes who spoil the fruits. The other way false prophets spoil the fruit is that they do not equip God's people to stand (endure) in the battle (compare 1 Cor. 14:8). Contrarily, the Church must be prepared to stand in the **faith** of Jesus, even during the great pressure (Rev. 14:10-20). But! But! How will the Church stand in the great hardship?

The Church will stand in faith, because the Church will **know**, in a short time, the Lord will come (Rev. 16:14-15). Jesus is the author of our faith, and **He will be there** with the Church all the way through until the end of the pressure. Thus, He is also the "perfecter (or completer) of our faith" (see Heb. 12:2-4, **NIV**) — as it is written, "I am Alpha and Omega, the beginning and the **ending**" (Rev. 1:8, KJV). He **is** the "ending." Stand, therefore, having your loins girt about with truth, resisting the lying power of Satan.

Satan, through the false prophet, and his "foxes" is sending a false anointing to seduce people. The subtle message is "believe the lie." Worship the creature instead of the creator. Take heed to yourselves that you do not lose your reward, by listening to **seducers in men.** In these days, men shall see false prophets moving in wonders of falsehood. They will be following **"energies."** The grass root of this is the New Age movement.

They shall mysteriously mutate themselves into sheep's clothing, **trying** to enter in among us. However, thank God that Jesus has true prophets with eyes of the dove (compare S.S. 1:5; Matt. 3:16). These prophets are those who were once called seers.

These seers, through the Seven Spirits of God, who are in His people, are exposing the falsehood. They are exposing the unseen lawless power at work within the false prophets. It is this invisible realm that will be open to you in the next chapter. One will understand what really exists in the unseen.

Chapter 3
Dominion in the Unseen

Rom. 1:20, KJV:
*For the **invisible** things of him from the creation of the world are clearly seen, being **understood** by the things that are made, even his eternal power and Godhead; so that they are without excuse:*

In the invisible world of the authority of darkness, there exist many rulers. These rulers include kings who have a domain. There are also dominions in the invisible who dominate or control, certain things. Principalities or beginnings also exist in the invisible. All these are under some authority (i.e., the authority of Satan). Jesus created them for a specific **function** before they fell.

Col. 1:16, KJV:
*For by him were all things created, that are in heaven, and that are in earth, visible and invisible, whether they be **thrones, or dominions, or principalities, or powers**: all things were created by him, and for him:*

Eph. 6:12, NIV:
*For our struggle is not against flesh and blood, but against the rulers, against the **authorities,** against the **powers** of this dark world and against the spiritual forces of evil in the heavenly realms.*

As one can see, in the invisible realm there are orders just like in the visible world. Paul, in the verse above distinguishes between "flesh and blood" rulers, and rulers in the heavenly. "For the **invisible** things of him from the creation of the world are clearly seen, being **understood** by the things that are made, even his **eternal power** and **Godhead;** so that they are without excuse" (Rom. 1:20, KJV).

Before I discuss the false prophet-the **dominion** in the unseen it is appropriate that I give a brief understanding of the invisible hierarchy of darkness. It is important to understand the full weight of the operations of darkness, especially the dominion **(controller)** angels.

King Angels

Among these unseen angels, the first is what the Scripture calls **thrones** (Col. 1:16). Kings sit upon thrones, and there exist many **king angels**. The Church has thought that Satan is the only king angel in the authority of darkness. However, do not be deceived, there exists **king death, and kings of Persia** (Dan. 10:13). There is **king Abaddon** (Rev. 9:11); there is also **king leviathan** (Job 41:1; 34); and **king Heylel.** They are among the kings in the unseen realm. Satan himself has "seven heads" who wore crowns when referred to in Revelations.

Rev. 12:3, KJV:
*And there appeared another wonder in heaven; and behold a great red dragon, having **seven heads** and ten horns, and **seven crowns** upon his heads.*

Satan holds or controls these heads. It is also significant to know that kings wear "crowns." Therefore, these "heads" had "crowns." In the book of Hebrews, we learn that Satan "had" **(lit., held)** the power of death (Heb. 2:14). This truth also demonstrates why Satan is also called Prince of <u>**devils.**</u> (Matt. 12:24).

Satan "had" the power of death, but Jesus **now** holds the keys of death and hell. However, death is still a king angel, whose power Satan can use. The person of death rules in the areas of death, plagues, hunger, the sword, the wild beasts of the earth and

terror. Death is a king because he is called the **"king** of terrors" (Job 18).

In like manner, the angel Abaddon is called **king** of the bottomless pit. In the book of Job, the writer talks about king death in relation to the fate of the wicked. Even though Job's friends were wrongly calling him wicked, there is truth in their statements, especially concerning the angelic realm.

Job 18:11-14, KJV:
*[11]**Terrors** shall make him afraid on every side, and shall drive him to his feet. [12]His strength shall be **hungerbitten,** and destruction shall be ready at his side.[13]It shall devour the strength of his skin: even the firstborn of **death** shall devour his strength. [14]His confidence shall be rooted out of his tabernacle, and it shall bring him to the **king of terrors.***

The writer in Job uses words like, "the firstborn of death" (part of which is terror) "hunger bitten" and the **"king of terrors"** (death himself). As one can see, king death sits enthroned upon these things. Listen to what John saw in his vision.

Rev. 6:8, KJV:
*And I looked, and behold a pale horse: and **his name** that sat on him was **Death,** and Hell followed with him. And power was given unto them over the fourth part of the earth, to kill with **sword,** and with **hunger,** and with **death (or plague),** and with the **beasts** of the earth.*

Death is enthroned over the sword, hunger (famine), plagues, and over the beasts of the earth. There is a lot more concerning king death that I could elaborate on, but this will suffice for the purpose it was intended.

Time will also not permit me to discuss king Abaddon, king leviathan, and the kings of Persia; except to say that king Abaddon is "the angel of (out of) the bottomless pit," whose name means, "to destroy utterly." Concerning king leviathan it is written, "He beholdeth all **high** things: he is a **king** over all the children of **pride**" (Job 41:34).

The kings of Persia are plural because of the two nations they rule, which are Media and Persia (Dan. 5:28; 9:1: 10:1). These are just some among the thrones in the unseen realm. Nevertheless, as stated before, Satan is the prince of some of these angels. In the words of John, they are "his" angels (Rev. 12:7). Jesus also called the devils that followed Satan, Satan also.

Satan, the Prince of satans

Matt. 12:24-26, KJV:
*24But when the Pharisees heard it, they said, This fellow doth not cast out devils, but by Beelzebub the prince of the devils. 25And Jesus knew their thoughts, and said unto them, Every kingdom divided against itself is brought to desolation; and every city or house divided against itself shall not stand: 26And if **Satan** cast out **Satan,** he is divided against himself; how shall then his kingdom stand?*

Jesus calls the followers of Satan (prince of devils) Satan, also. The principle is that Satan is not just one entity. Satan, in reality, consists of Satan himself and many Satan(s) (devils). There is Satan—prince of devils and there is Satan—other devils. In the word of Revelation, Satan has seven heads, or seven other Satan(s) that are heads. But they are considered as one Satan. Do you see it? The Scripture reveals that Satan's seven heads are seven kings, **visible and invisible.**

This is demonstrated in the crowns they wear (Rev. 12:3). The book of Revelation makes known this truth, when the angel explains to John what he had seen in Chapter 17. There are seven landmasses, or continents, which the Scripture calls **mountains** (Rev. 17:9). For example, the whole landmass the continent of

America is on is the **head** of a mountain. The mountain bottom is covered under the oceans. That is why the further out a person goes in the water, the deeper it gets. We live on a "crown" of a mountain. Each of the seven "crowns" rules a continent (Rev. 12:3 w/Rev. 17:9).

This mountaintop, or continent, is ruled by one of the seven heads, whether it is Satan himself, or other king angels. Or, should I say, other Satan(s). Seven is **representative** of all the ruling heads. This means, in reality, there are more than seven nations. Thus, Satan's seven heads are representative of all the principalities who rule a particular nation. Satan may be the wisest king angel (Ezek. 28); but he might not be the fiercest (Matt. 12:45); neither is he the only ruling angel that exists (Eph. 6:12).

Rulers of This Dark Age

It is the powers that rule this dark age that we wrestle against. *"For our struggle is not against flesh and blood, but against the rulers, against the **authorities**, against the **powers** of this dark world..." (Eph. 6:12, NIV)*. These powers can't work, except an authority sanctions them.

Thus, there exists authority in the realm of darkness. Satan is the authority among his angels. But there exists also the authority of the air (Eph. 2), among the other authorities of darkness. They are all governed by principalities (lit., **beginnings,** governments, chiefs, rulers).

Principalities are also governed by principles (rules of actions). This reveals that even though these angels are transgressors against God, there exist confederated principles among them. In the words of Jesus if they are divided they can't stand.

It is by these chief principles, coupled with powers and authorities, angels attempt to **dominate** this present age. Our Job is to counter their activity by prayer and fasting, binding the principalities; then spoil Satan's house. I could remark more extensively about powers, authorities, and principalities, but it would take us too far off our topic at hand, which is the dominion angel (Col. 1:16).

Controlling Spirits

The understanding of dominion angels is very important. This will help you to gain understanding concerning the work of the false prophet. **Dominion literally means mastery, controller, and lordship.** When God created the earth, He also created angels for Himself (Col. 1:16). They are to **control** certain conditions on the earth. There are God's "elect angels" (I Tim. 5:21) who control, or have mastery over the wind, the sea, the waters, the **times** etc. **Again, for emphasis, this is only as the Lord commands.** Let's note some of these examples in the Scripture. I will start first in the book of Revelation.

Rev. 7:1, KJV:
*And after these things I saw **four angels** standing on the four corners of the earth, **holding** the **four winds** of the earth, that the wind should not blow on the earth, nor on the sea, nor on any tree.*

One can see here that the four angels had the ability to control the wind that it **"should not blow"** on the earth. However, I would like to reiterate that God gives the commands. He is in total control (Ps. 103:20). There is the angel of the **waters** (Rev. 16:1-5). John also saw "another angel came out from the altar, which had power (lit.,; authority) over fire..." (Rev. 14:18). There is **Rahab**, the **dragon** of the sea (Ps. 89:8-10, Isaiah 51:9, Job 9:13; 26:12).

He rages in the sea; when the waves thereof arise. There is one who **controls** this controller. His name is Jesus (Luke 8:24-25). "⁹Thou rulest the raging of the sea: when the waves thereof arise, thou stillest them. ¹⁰ Thou hast **broken Rahab** in pieces, as one that is slain; thou hast scattered thine enemies with thy strong arm" (Ps. 89:9-10, KJV).

There are angels created by Jesus who can control circumstances on this earth (Job 7:12). Though some of the fallen ones seem to get out of control, by being rebellious, they are still under the authority of Jesus. "Who is gone into heaven, and is on the right hand of God; angels and authorities and powers being made subject unto him" (1 Pet. 3:22, KJV). Some of these angels are called **earthly** spirits. They were created **on the** earth, and for Adam to **help** Adam do his work on the earth.

Created to Help; Fell to Cause Adversity

1 John 4:6, KJV:
We are of God: he that knoweth God heareth us; he that is not of God heareth not us. Hereby know we the spirit of truth, and the spirit of error.

Now, when I say **earthly** spirit, I mean in the sense that some angelic beings are of the **planet** earth. The Scripture says that there exists a spirit **of** error. When something is "of" something, it means, it is from that particular thing (genitive case). So, there is a spirit **of** error. The word **error** is the Greek word "plane;"and it is used in the feminine.³ The word is also defined as "a wandering," from whence we get our word planet. Therefore, the spirit **of** "plane" can be the "spirit **of planet**." What planet? The planet **earth!** In the Interlinear Bible this is the structure: to

---

³*I am aware that gender is not significant when referring to inanimate things, however relative to Scriptures; God also uses gender relative to apparent spiritless entities.*

pneuma tes plane which translates—the spirit the error. The Young's literal translation says the same thing.

The phrase **"tes plane"** is important. This is because the word "planetes," (Strong's #4107) used in Jude 13 of **"wandering stars" (lit., planet stars)** is constructed from these two words. Except, **"tes (the)"** is at the end of the word plane in Jude 13 **(plane-tes)**, while **"tes (the)"** is before the word "plane" in 1 John 4:6 **(tes plane)**. They are both saying the same thing. As a result, the phrase the spirit of error could be translated the spirit of the planet. The King James left out the definite article "the" (tes).

The point is this-the spirit of error is literally "the spirit of the error" which **can** be interpreted to mean "the spirit of the planet (earth)." The word "plane" is feminine in gender; and we know from Scripture the earth is always referred to as "her" (Rev. 12:16). **An** understanding is that the **feminine "plane"** is the **earth.** From this, one can see more clearly an explication from the book of Genesis. One will be able to see the original design of God **in when, for whom,** and **from where** he made the beasts of the field, or, literally, the living creatures of the flat field.

The Lord had created heaven and earth. But the earth was without form and void (vacuity). He then proceeded to do several power acts by separating the light from the darkness; creating the firmament; the gathering of the waters, the growth of the herbs; the lights of the firmament; the living soul of the earth, etc. Then he made another creation: He made man, in the beauty of God's image. After all these creations, God saw that Adam was alone. God proceeded to make, **yet further,** what the Scripture calls a **"help meet."** This literally means **"an aid; to surround, to protect, to help."** With this in mind, let's look to the Scriptures.

Gen. 2:18, KJV:
*And the LORD God said, It is not good that the man should be alone; I will make him an **help meet** for him.*

We see that God wanted to make Adam an aid for him. So, whatever God is about to make - it, they, or she - will be to aid Adam. But, if you will note the first things God created were living creatures, fowls of the air, etc. These were the first aids for Adam the Lord made. And the Lord made them from the **earth.**

Gen. 2:19, KJV:
*And **out of the ground** the LORD God formed every **beast of the field,** and every **fowl of the air;** and brought them unto Adam to see what he would call them: **and** whatsoever Adam called every living creature, that was the name thereof.*

As one can readily see, the first thing God made, after he wanted to give Adam a help meet, were every beast **(lit., living creature)** of the field (Compare Ezek. 1) and every fowl of the air (compare Mk. 4:4 w/Mk.4:15); **not** the woman as some would affirm. Also—notice! It was **out of the ground** the Lord made these new orders of living creatures, not in heaven, but from this earth.

They are called spirits of error, (or spirits of the planet—which I interpret to mean the planet earth). Nevertheless, God wanted to see what Adam would call each one, and name them along with **every other** "living creature" (lit., living soul).

Adam did **name** them; but he did not **call** them a helpmeet. God was waiting to see if Adam would **call** them a helpmeet. In fact, Adam found none among the mute animals nor the beasts of the field that he wanted to call his helpmeet.

Gen. 2:20, KJV:
*And Adam gave names to all cattle, and to the fowl of the air, and to every beast of the field; but for Adam there was not **found** an help meet for him.*

Do you see it? Adam gave them names, but he did not <u>call</u> them a helpmeet. Also, among these living creatures he **"found"** none that qualified to be his aid, or companion. Note: Adam rejected bestiality. Nonetheless, the interpretation is this: God wanted someone to aid Adam. He proceeded to make some more living creatures out of the **ground** of the garden, because the man was in the garden at this time. These beings were created after those of Genesis 1:20-23. The Septuagint bears this truth out.

Gen. 2:18, Septuagint:
*And God formed **yet farther** out of the earth all the wild beast of the fields, and all the birds of the sky, and he brought them to Adam, to see what he would call them, and whatever Adam called any living creature, that was the name of it.*

The Septuagint says, "And God formed **yet farther**" (emphasis supplied by the author). The next question is from where were they made? According to the Septuagint, they came "out of the earth" Yes! God continued to form or make "yet farther out of the earth." In other words, "yet farther" means He did some **"original"** making of these particular creatures after Genesis 1:20-23. Do you see it now? The **serpent** was among these **beasts of field**, or living creatures of the field (Gen. 3:1). John called him "that **old** serpent, called the devil."

Rev. 12:9, KJV:
*And the great dragon was cast out, that **old** serpent, called the Devil, and Satan, which deceiveth the whole world: he was cast out into the earth, and his angels were cast out with him.*

The word **"old"** literally means **original.** The "old serpent" is the "original" serpent - literally—that is the devil. He is the original one from Genesis 3:1 to the end of his life in the book of Revelation.

The serpent, in Genesis, is called a beast of the field, (lit., living creature) **not "cattle"** (a mute beast of Gen. 2:20). This beast of the field, along with the fowls of the air, can **talk** (compare Gen. 3:1, KJV; Rev. 8:13, NIV or A.S. Worrel Translation). This makes him of a higher order than the cattle.

That order is the order of Cherubim God caused to come into being in the Garden of God, to serve Adam (Gen. 2; Ezek. 28:13; 14). Cherubim can talk (compare Ezek. 1; Ezek 10 with Rev. 4:8; Isaiah 6:1-3). The serpent talked—thus making him not a "cattle"—mute beast—but a living creature—Cherub (Gen. 3:1, Ezek. 1).

Therefore, the first set of help meets, or **aids that** the Lord made for Adam came from the **ground** of the Garden of Eden upon the **earth.** Hence, they are called spirits of error (plane), or, should I say, spirits of the planet **(earth).** They probably came to be known as spirits of error in a negative sense, because they caused Adam and Eve to **err or wander** from God.

Adam did not **call** this order of creation the Lord had made to be along his side. He **"called"** Eve (Gen. 2:23). In fact Adam says, "This is **now (finally)** bones of my bones and flesh of my flesh; she shall be **called** woman" (Gen. 2:23). I believe this created a bitter envy and pride in the heart of the devil and his cohorts. The hate became so deep, he caused them to **sin,** err, or wander, from God's counsel. Thus, spirits of the planet **(error, wandering: compare Job 1:7)** has an evil connotation with it.

As can be understood from these scriptures, the living creatures were originally created on the earth to <u>aid</u> Adam. They were **intended** to make the man's work less in force or degree. They were to aid, help, protect, and surround Adam in every way. That is why I said, 'They were created on the **earth,** and for Adam to **help** <u>utilize</u> the elements on the earth.' These are those whom the Scripture now calls Satan and his angels (Rev. 12:7-9; Matt. 25:41). They were made on the earth to help manage the earth under Adam's leadership, through God (See Chapter three for further development of living creatures).

Violent Rain

The false prophet, who is an **earthly** spirit, has to do with things of the heavens, even though his abode is under the earth. He causes fire to come down from **heaven** on the earth (Rev. 13; compare Job 1). He also **seems** to influence the operation of the <u>violent rain</u> that descends from heaven by God's command (Gen. 8:1). **Note:** This should be no surprise. When it comes to judging mankind, for whatever reasons, fallen angels are quick to respond (Job 1-2; Ps. 78:49). Daniel the prophet saw some aspects of this rain allegorically.

Dan. 7:11, KJV:
*I beheld then because of the voice of the great words which the horn spake: I beheld even till the beast was slain, and his **body** destroyed, and given to the burning flame.*

In this verse of Daniel, the prophet saw the **"body (lit., geshem)"** of the beast destroyed. As one will see, this is not **just** the "body" of the beast, but it also points to something else. The word "geshem" literally means to rain hard or violently with a secondary meaning of "body (prob. for the figurative idea of a HARD rain)" (Strong's #1654, 1655, and 1652). With this in mind, we will take a look at some stunning truths about this <u>geshem</u> from the books of Nehemiah and Ezra.

We learned from Dan. 7:11 that <u>geshem</u> is associated with the first beast to come (Dan. 7:11; Rev. 13:1-2). Daniel 7:11 could read, "I beheld then because of the voice of the great words which the horn spake:" I beheld even till the beast was slain and **his violent rain** destroyed and given to the burning flames."

Yes! The beast's violent rain will be burned. Is this a **metaphor** Daniel is seeing? I believe so. Most of the chapter is **allegorical.** In a **figure of speech** God was hiding this mystery until the time of the end (Dan. 12:9). It is now time for the book to be opened. This is done by no other than **the Lamb** himself, Jesus, in us (Rev. 5; Col. 1:27; 1 Cor. 2:12).

Geshem, the Enemy

The Lord began to increase my understanding of <u>geshem</u> in the early 1990's. I understood how he is associated with rain, in the spirit. This was accomplished from the books of Nehemiah and Ezra. Let us hear the words of the book.

Neh. 6:1-2, KJV:
*¹Now it came to pass, when Sanballat, and Tobiah, and **Geshem** the Arabian, and the **rest of our enemies,** heard that I had builded the wall, and that there was no breach left therein; (though at that time I had not set up the doors upon the gates;) ²That Sanballat and **Geshem** sent unto me, saying, Come, let us meet together in some one of the villages in the plain of Ono. But they thought to do me mischief.*

Neh. 2:19, KJV:
*But when Sanballat the Horonite, and Tobiah the servant, the Ammonite, and **Geshem the Arabian,** heard it, they laughed us to*

scorn, and despised us, and said, What is this thing that ye do? will ye rebel against the king?

In these verses we understand Geshem (a man) to be among enemies of the Jews (Neh. 6:1). The book of Daniel associated Geshem, in parable form, with the beast. He is also said to be an Arabian. Arabian means "mixed," or "mingle" in the Hebrew language.

Thus it can point to all the mixed religions that will be an enemy of the Church. But it also prophetically points to the Muslim religion that was birthed in Arabia. Ever since the days of Ishmael, Abraham's son by the Egyptian, there has been animosity between the Jews, and the sons of Ishmael. **Yet there is hope through Jesus.**

However, **spiritually** speaking, Geshem the Arabian, the enemy of the Jews, is also the enemy of the Church (Rom. 2:28). **Note: This is in no wise saying that Muslims or Arabians can't be saved (see Acts 2:6-11; 2:37)**. Yet the false prophet is the spirit behind the Muslim religion, not Gabriel as claimed.

One of the false prophet's form is as geshem (Arabic based religion), and allegorically, he is **raining** violently his false teachings on the world. I believe one of the major oppositions the Church will face will be the Islamic religion in its many forms.

The Muslim religion, as we know it in America, is not the true nature of Islam, or, should I say, they are not publicly showing their true belief. Originally, Islam was not a religious form, as we know it. When it was first established, the whole purpose was, by military might, to conquer every nation until they became Muslims. Thus, once a nation became Muslim they would do the same thing also--conquer other nations. This concept is still taught in the Islamic nations.

Their purpose is to make it accepted worldwide. However, it is not publicly done by force now,[4] but by the power of money. Billions of dollars are being spent to spread Islam each year. One of the false prophet's major religions on the earth will be Islamic in nature. This truth is **written in type** in the books of Nehemiah, Ezra and Daniel.

Now, one can see the weight of Daniel's chapter seven, verse eleven. The "body" of the beast is actually "geshem;" or, in the metaphor of Nehemiah, Geshem, the Islamic movement; and all mixed religions that will be the enemy of the Church.

If you notice, "the beast was slain, and his **body (Hebrew geshem)** destroyed, and given to the burning flame" (Dan. 7:11). In Revelation 19:20, it was both the beast and **the false prophet** (geshem **in type)** that was thrown in the lake of fire.

In a figure of speech, the false prophet, alias geshem, is causing violent rain to come down. It is a rain of deception. The deception will rain so relentlessly, it will be hard for men to separate themselves from its effects. The book of Ezra exemplifies this very well.

Be You Separated Unto God

In the days of Ezra the people had **divorced** their Jewish wives. They joined themselves to women of other nations who served other gods (Ezra 10; 10-11; 1 Tim. 4:1-3; Mal. 2:11-15). But upon demand it was hard for the people to separate themselves from these strange wives—Babylon's daughters (Rev. 17:5).

---

[4] *Certainly, terrorism is not being excluded.*

Ezra 10:10-11, KJV:
*¹⁰And Ezra the priest stood up, and said unto them, Ye have transgressed, and have taken strange wives, to increase the trespass of Israel. ¹¹Now therefore make confession unto the LORD God of your fathers, and do his pleasure: and **separate** yourselves from the people of the land, and from the strange wives.*

Ezra 10:13, KJV:
*But the people are many, and it is a **time of much rain (lit a time of geshem)**, and we are not able to **stand without (lit; stand separate)**, neither is this a work of one day or two: for we are many that have transgressed in this thing.*

This is what will also happen in the last days. **Geshem**, the false prophet, will be on the scene. It will be the **time of geshem**. He will cause many to marry **strange** doctrines (I Tim. 4:1). When God calls for a separation, it will be difficult. Some will not be able to **"stand separate,"** because it will be a time of **much rain**. This is one of the ways the "falling away" will manifest itself. It is geshem's **time** and he, allegorically, is raining waters of false doctrines. Every false religion is from this false prophet. But I say, take heed and watch the **rain** of Islam.

Figuratively speaking, the rain cloud of Islam shall cover the earth and the false prophet shall cause his doctrine to rain violently. The result—men will believe the lie over the truth. Men across the world will be converted to Islam. Behold, I show you a mystery. The first beast shall be known for "understanding dark sentences." **This can be interpreted as understanding scriptures (Dan. 8:23; Pr. 1:1-6).** This is significant.

The world at large will believe the Islamic movement. They will mix their doctrine with the holy writ, giving false understanding of what is written. Or the Islamic beliefs will seem close to the Bible. As stated above, the word Arabia in Scripture also means to mix or mingle. Geshem, the controller of the rain of deception—

but not without permission (Job. 1:9-12, 16; 19; Job 2:4-6; **Rev. 17:17**)—shall wander across the earth propagandizing his message, mixed with the word of God.

Then the beast who shall **understand Scriptures**, "through his policy" (lit., wisdom, intelligence) shall cause craft to prosper in his hand (Dan. 8:25). He shall deceive the world, and wittingly blaspheme the Lord of heaven. Geshem, **allegorically**, points to the work of the false prophet in raining deception. This earthly spirit can rain false doctrines. **He violently rains** that which causes error upon the earth. The Scripture calls him the spirit of error.

Wandering Stars

As noted before, the word "error" is the Greek word plane and planao, which also means **to wander**, deceive, **or seduce**. These Greek words are where we get our English word planet (Gk., planetes); hence, **wandering spirits**—in the words of the King James version, **"seducing spirits,"** (1Tim. 4:1).

These are earthly spirits originally created to help man. Except now, they work in false prophets. "Woe unto them! For they have gone in the way of Cain, and ran greedily after the error ("plane"-wandering) of Balaam" (Jude 11). Balaam is a false prophet, alias soothsayer (Joshua 13:22).

Jude also called these false prophets "wandering stars" (Jude 13). This segment of the verse literally reads "planet stars." The prophets are the planet ("planetes") stars, and it is the seducing ("planao") spirits that cause them to wander. These spirits also dominate the false prophets. **In other words, they are possessed by spirits of wandering**.

The earth rotates, or **wanders** around the sun. So likewise, these "planao"(wandering) spirits cause the false prophets to wander about—for the word seducing also mean, "to wander about" (see Job 1:7). The spirit of error ("plane": wanderer, seducer) is the antichrist, alias false prophet, that shall come into the world. He is among the controllers, or seducing spirits in false prophets. His purpose is to seduce (cause to wander) men from the Christ.

Seduction

1 John 2:18-20, KJV:
*[18] Little children, it is the last time: and as ye have heard that **antichrist** shall come, **even now** are there many antichrists; **whereby** we know that it is the last time. [19]They went out from us, but they were not of us; for if they had been of us, they would no doubt have continued with us: but they went out, that they might be made manifest that they were not all of us. [20]But ye have an unction from the Holy One, and ye know all things.*

1 John 2:26, KJV:
*These things have I written unto you concerning them that **seduce** you.*

2 John 7
*For many **deceivers (or seducers)** are entered into the world, who confess not that Jesus Christ is come in the flesh. This is a **deceiver (or seducer)** and an antichrist.*

These seducers shall enter into the world from the unseen. The false prophet is the leader of these seducers. The purpose of the false prophet is to gain the **mastery** over his targets that he might seduce them from the true anointed one (The Christ). His desire is to replace the anointing which ye have received with his anointing; for antichrist means "instead of Christ," or "against Christ."

The false prophet wants to place his anointing in you instead of Christ's anointing, which you have. Are you with me so far? He, the false prophet, causes **divorce,** or falling away from the true Christ and he **tries to rejoin** the person to his anointing by influences.

Wrong Influence

He dominates his subjects by the subtlety of influence. Because he is a controlling spirit, he automatically tries to dominate and seduce you from following the true Christ. The book of Revelation teaches that he "deceiveth" (lit., cause to wander or roam) them that dwell on the earth to worship the beast. He deceives by **influence.** Thus, **by influence,** he is **controlling.** Let us see how his influence dominates.

Rev. 13:13-14, KJV:
*13And he doeth great wonders, so that **he maketh fire come down from heaven** on the earth in the sight of men, 14And deceiveth them that dwell on the earth by the means of those miracles which he had power to do in the sight of the beast; saying to them that dwell on the earth, that they should make an image to the beast, which had the wound by a sword, and did live.*

The false prophet uses the influence of signs and wonders to control. He fooled the people of the earth so effectively he says, "to them that dwell on the earth, that they should make an image to the beast" (Rev. 13:14b). He gained the **mastery** over them, to the point of deceiving men to take the mark of the beast. We as believers must remember, he is a **master** of **controlling by deception**. He works in the unseen to control situations in the "seen." He will scheme circumstances or destroy situations to cause his prophecies to come to pass (i.e., miracle of fire from heaven).

He "plane" (wanders) from place to place; to make sure his false declarations are substantiated. Even though God can frustrate him, He permits this to happen (Isaiah 44:25, NIV with 2 Thess. 2:11). There is going to be a full force of dominion spirits released **into** the earth from the realm of spirit (1 Tim. 4:1-3; 2 John 1:7-8). Their purpose is to seduce and control the earth, and them that dwell therein. They shall influence mankind to love the world more than God. The world will seem to be livelier than God. These seducers in men must not deceive the Church.

The Friendship of the World

1 John 4:1, KJV:
*Beloved, believe not every **spirit**, but try the spirits whether they are of God: because many false prophets are gone out into the **world**.*

1 John 4:5, KJV:
*They are of the **world:** therefore speak they of the world, and the world hears them.*

1 John 2:16, KJV:
*For all that is in the **world**, the lust of the flesh, and the lust of the eyes, and the pride of life, is not of the Father, but is of the world.*

False prophets will propagandize the world in the area of things that the flesh lusts after; things persons possess that he or she can be proud of; and whatever their eyes lust after (or covet)they can have especially things that can be brought or sold (Rev. 13:17). All this will be given for a small price (Rev. 13:16).

The false prophet will then give signs and wonders to bear witness to the worldly declarations. These signs are produced by his **deceptive** power. The miracles are the icing on the cake; because most people will not believe unless they see signs and wonders (John 4:48). Jesus says, however, "An **evil** and **adulterous** generation seeketh after a sign" (Matt. 12:39).

I encourage all of you; do not follow signs, and wonders, **if** they lead you to love the world and the things therein (Rev. 13; 1 John 2:16; James 4:4). The false prophet's signs are a strong **delusion (lit., plane - a wandering).** He will use his **illusions** to control the world to receive him, and the first beast. He desires to gain the **control,** the **lordship** and the **mastery** over any that will believe his lies (compare 2 Tim. 2:26).

His purpose is to **control in** the unseen first-via false prophets. Then he will manifest himself literally in the seen. He will be declaring his message, which is, "believe the lie over the truth." It is this manifestation of him in the visible we will discuss in the next chapter. You will understand whether or not the false prophet will be seen as a man, angel or beast.

Chapter 4
Man or Beast

Rev. 13:11, KJV:
And I beheld another beast coming up out of the earth; and he had two horns like a lamb, and he spake as a dragon.

While I was contemplating on what title to assign to this chapter, I felt impressed to name it "Man or Beast?" This title focuses on one of the mysteries that surround the **false prophet**. Is he a beast, angel or a man; or is he all of these? Let us see.

The book of Revelation is an **open** book for, the angel says to John, "**seal not** the saying of the prophecy of this book: For the **time** is at hand" (Rev. 22:10). Apostles and prophets have the ability to seal, or open revelations that God has given to them (Rev. 22:10, Dan. 12:4).

However, the mysteries of the book of Revelation were appointed to remain open. It is a book full of mystery. Yet every mystery is **open** to him that has an ear to hear. It is in this book we get a glimpse of the manifestations of the false prophet, alias, **another beast**.

The Scripture says this beast **speaks as** a dragon. The word **as** is the Greek word "hos" (hoce), which means **"which how."** **Hos** is from a root word that means who, which, what, that (Strong's #5613, #3739). So, this phrase could read: "he spoke **which how** a dragon;" meaning he **"which"** (is) a dragon spoke **"how?"** He spoke **"as"** a dragon! In other words, he spoke **as** a dragon because, in reality, he **is** a dragon. This beast, though, is deceptive; he is dressed **like** a sheep.

Dressed Like a Sheep

"Beware of false prophets, which come to you in **sheep's clothing**, but inwardly they are ravening wolves" (Matt. 7:15). Jesus says false prophets would come in sheep's **clothing**. Jesus did not say the false prophets would come as sheep, but **in** "sheep's **clothing**." Clothing literally means apparel, and it points to the sheep's wool (hair)—symbolic of "covering" and "glory" (Compare 1 Cor.11:15a).

Glory means good opinion and estimate (Vines). Therefore, false prophets will come clothed in **glory—good opinion or good estimate**. Understand a mystery. Part of the glory—good opinion—of the Lamb of God is the beauty of the **seven horns**, and **seven eyes** which clothed Him (Rev. 5:6). It was not a natural beauty[5]:" and when we shall see him, there is **no beauty** that we should desire him" (Isaiah 53:2).

The **seven horns** and eyes are the **seven Spirits of God** (Rev. 5:6). The Spirit of God is He who brings glory—good opinion—to the Father, by His complete power, sight and gentleness (Luke 7:12-16). Therefore the false prophet's "two horns"—Rev. 13:11—will create a facade of a "good opinion" for himself. "Two horns" show the false prophet's **limited** power, compared to "**seven**"—**complete, or all power** of the true Lamb (Rev. 5:6; Matt. 28:18).

The false prophet will come with limited power of a lamb. He will come in a **counterfeit** spirit of God. But, we know that his scheme of appearing to be "good" is false, according to the Spirit of God (1 Cor. 12: 10-11). Even though, he may look like a sheep

---

[5] *See my book The Lamb. I dedicated an entire chapter to the Lamb's ugliness and its applications to us.*

outwardly, inwardly he is a **dragon,** for "he spoke **as** a dragon," meaning nothing good comes out of his mouth.

Mutation

I gained more understanding of the mystery of the second beast about four years ago. My wife and I were in a season of intensified prayer and study. It was about four or five in the morning, after watching and studying. I laid down to rest when I was immediately caught up in a vision of God. I saw a red dragon and I in the heat of a battle.

We wrestled to the ground, and then the fighting ceased for a moment. I then ascended again to the heavens, and the red dragon followed me. In his pursuit of me, I turned towards him to battle, and fire came out of my mouth and devoured him. **[Note:** I believe the fire is symbolic of the word of God consuming the false prophet(s) (Jer. 23:29)**].**

The beast then fell to the ground as dead; but he wasn't. As I descended to the earth again, to my surprise, he had mutated into a man or angel. His appearance was that of a man, but he had two horns like a **male lamb** beside his ears. As the vision continued, I realized who the red dragon was that I was wrestling against. He was the **false prophet** himself, who had mutated back into a **mixed man.** The **man, or angel** with the **lamb's** horn, was, in reality, a **dragon beast.**

Angelic Beasts

An understanding of the mystery is that some spirit beings are **beasts.** Satan is also a dragon **beast.** In Ezekiel 28, we learn that Satan is the **cherub** being discussed, even though the chapter could point to someone else.

Ezek. 28:14, NIV:
*You were anointed as a guardian **cherub**, for so I ordained you. You were on the holy mount of God; you walked among the fiery stones.*

Ezek. 28:14, KJV:
*Thou art the anointed **cherub** that covereth; I have set thee so: thou was upon the holy mountain of God; thou hast walked up and down in the midst of the stones of fire.*

In Ezekiel 1, we learn that some cherubim have **four faces.** Satan is said to have "seven heads," But note, he has **four** names, or **faces** (Rev. 12:14; Rev. 20:2). It is common among cherubim to have more than one head or faces.

Ezek. 1:5-6, KJV:
*⁵Also out of the midst thereof came the likeness of four **living creatures.** And this is their appearance; they had the likeness of a man. ⁶And every one had **four faces,** and every one had four wings.*

These four faced cherubim were also called **living creatures.** This is significant because these are not quite the same as **mute** beasts (the faces of which these cherubim possess). The serpent or Satan that was in the **Garden of Eden** was also called a **living creature.**

Gen. 3:1, KJV:
*Now the serpent was more subtle than any **beast (lit., living creature) of the field** which the Lord God had made. And he said unto the woman, yea, hath God said, Ye shall not eat of every tree of the garden?*

The living creatures of Ezekiel's book had the face of a lion, eagle, man, and ox. All of these are beasts except one, a man. The dragon or Satan has seven heads, but four faces. One of the faces of the dragon is a serpent.

Rev. 12:14, KJV:
*And to the woman were given two wings of a great eagle, that she might fly into the wilderness, into her place, where she is nourished for a time, and times, and half a time, from the **face** of the serpent.*

The point is this, cherubim are called living creatures, the same word for beast, in Genesis 3:1. They also have beastly faces, and some of them are **beasts** (i.e., Satan). Satan the cherub is a **dragon beast**. The "first beast" is **mostly** a **leopard** beast in a man, or a leopard-like kingdom; and the false prophet is a **mixed beast** (i.e., **man, dragon, lamb's horn**).

The cherubim were man-like in appearance, yet had the faces of beasts (Ezek. 1). The false prophet is also a beast. Yet he can mutate into a **man's** figure, or visa-versa. Daniel called Gabriel, an archangel, a man.

Dan. 9:21, KJV:
*Yea, whiles I was speaking in prayer, even the **man Gabriel**, whom I had seen in the vision at the beginning, being caused to fly swiftly, touched me about the time of the evening oblation.*

So, sometimes when the Scripture uses the word man, the man might be an angel (Ezek. 28; Dan. 9; Isaiah 14). Now that we have seen the beastly form of the false prophet, and others, I will give an interpretation of the mystery of how the false prophet will manifest himself.

Will the false prophet manifest himself physically as an angel? Will he possess a man? The answer lies within the title of the chapter: **Man or beast.** The understanding is that the false prophet is both.

According to 1 John 4 the spirit of antichrist **already possesses** some men (i.e., false prophets). Therefore, he has possessed some men, and will possess other men. Do not forget; he is a dominion in the unseen. The false prophet likes to control in the unseen, by possession. His ultimate desire, though, is to be seen. He shall "walk up out of the earth," physically; physically in the sense that as man he can see like a man and communicate. Likewise, men shall see the false prophet and have open fellowship with him.

Mankind Marrying Angels

Luke 17:26-27, KJV:
[26]And as it was in the days of Noe, so shall it be also in the days of the Son of man. [27]They did eat, they drank, **they married wives, they were given in marriage***, until the day that Noe entered into the ark, and the flood came, and destroyed them all.*

The Spirit of the Lord showed me that it was not just mankind who married in the day of Noah. The **angels** also married in those days.[6] They married women among mankind. In the words of Jesus, "they [women] were given in marriage."

Gen. 6:1-2, KJV:
[1]And it came to pass, when men began to multiply on the face of the earth, and **daughters** *were born unto them, [2]That the* **sons of God** *saw the daughters of men that they were fair; and they took them* **wives** *of all which they chose.*

They (the angels) left their house in heaven and came down to the earth to marry **"strange flesh"** [women] (see Jude 6-7). These angels visibly appeared to these women, and **slept** with them, physically, producing **giant** seed. Jesus declares that in the **days** when he comes, mankind will be doing the same thing.

Mankind will have open contact with fallen angels as a way of life. Angels will have intercourse with women again, producing

---

[6] *See my book Sex Pleasures for details.*

the same thing they did in the days of Noah. Sadly to say, a similarity to this sin is being manifested **in our day**—psychic, necromancy, medium, etc. In the latter time the world shall **worship** *(lit., kiss)* the dragon and the first beast because they shall manifest themselves physically for a time.

During the time, times, and half a time, the angels who transgressed, will not hesitate to **manifest** themselves. The dragon, the beast and the false prophet will do every wonder of falsehood to deceive the nations. The false prophet, among other angels, shall do as the other sons of God did. He shall live in and among men.

This mixed beast walked up **out of** the earth to be **on** the earth, that he might deceive the **earth, and** them that dwell **on** the earth (Rev. 13:11-14). Where are you dwelling, the **heavens,** the **sea,** or the **earth?** We who are in Christ dwell in the heavens (Eph. 2:6). Beasts-like men dwell upon the earth (compare Ecclesiastes 3:18-21).

Men with the Hearts of Beasts

Rev. 12:12, KJV:
*Therefore **rejoice, ye heavens,** and ye that **dwell** in them. **Woe** to the inhabiters of the **earth** and the **sea!** for the devil is come down onto you, having great wrath, because he knoweth that he hath but a short time.*

The book of Revelation spoke of three realms: **heaven, sea and earth.** It is from the sea of humanity and earthly realm that demonic beasts arise (Dan. 7; Rev. 13; James 3:15). The question is, shall the second beast **also** arise out of the earth **in** a man, or men? Yes!

The former exposition was his manifestation physically. Now you will understand how this beast operates in a person and/or persons. In the past, **beastly kings** and kingdoms arose out of the earth, and sea.

Dan. 7:2-3, KJV
*²Daniel spake and said, I saw in my vision by night, and behold, the four **winds (or spirits)** of heaven **strove (lit., gush forth)** upon the **great sea.** ³And four great beasts came up from the **sea**, diverse one from another.*

Here we see four **spirits** of heaven gushing forth on the great sea. The fact that they "gush forth" on the seas demonstrates that they **entered** the sea of humanity. A beast arising out of the sea follows this. Something similar happens in Revelation 13.

Rev. 13:1, NIV:
*And the dragon stood on the shore of the sea. And saw a beast **coming out of the sea.** He had ten horns and seven heads, with ten crowns on his horns, and on each head a blasphemous name.*

"The **dragon** stood on the shore of the **sea**." Then, the first beast arose out of the **sea**. This "**sea**" or "**great sea**" is the **sea of humanity**. The four spirits of heaven possessed four man beasts that came up from the sea of humanity. I use the term "man beast," because the Scripture teaches that these great beasts are four **kings** who shall arise out of the **earth** (Dan. 7:17).

The beasts are in kings. They came from the sea and earth. These men had the **hearts** of beasts, which point to the beasts in them (compare Dan. 7:4; 5:21). In Daniel Chapter seven, the lion, the bear, the leopard and the **metal beast** are all characteristic of the **spirits** in these kings and kingdoms. So, likewise, the beast that John saw in Rev. 13:11 can be characteristic of the spirit beast in a man.

The False Prophet, the Man

Rev. 13:11, KJV:
*And I beheld another beast coming up out of the **earth;** and he had two horns like a lamb, and he spake as a dragon.*

According to the Greek definitions, this should read, "And I beheld another beast **walking up out of** the earth." The fact that he walked up out of the earth is significant. It reveals the place **where** and **how** false prophets get their wisdom. There is a wisdom that does not come from **above.** This wisdom comes from **beneath** the **earth** (i.e., hell).

James 3:14-15, KJV:
*[14]But if you have bitter envying (lit., jealously; zeal) and strife in your hearts, glory not, and lie not against the truth. [15]This wisdom descendeth not from above, but is **earthly,** sensual, **devilish (lit., demonic).***

The false prophet walked up out of the **earth.** Beneath the earth is the place where the false prophet gets his "demonic" and "earthly" wisdom, or pseudo prophetic insight. This is **how** he (the false prophet—the man) illegally contacts the lawless spirits behind the secret of lawlessness (illegality). As noted in chapter one, the word mystery denotes that which is **known** by the initiated.

Therefore, for a man to communicate with these spirits (Satan, false prophet, etc.), he had to be initiated into the mystery of lawlessness. Thus, the initiated person is now possessed. This man, like his possessor, migrates **down**—beneath the earth, and **up**—knowingly (compare Isaiah 57:9). Thus, his prophetic wisdom is **earthly,** and **demonic.** (James 3:15) He will be full of **bitter** zeal (James 3:16) for the three (the dragon, the beast, and the false prophet).

The holy writ says, "**bitterness**" is the sin of divination" (literal rendition; 1 Sam. 15:23). This false prophet (the man) is bitter against God. Therefore, he is a diviner, as can be seen in I Sam. 15:23 (contrast Heb. 12:15). He is also a mature child of Satan (Act. 13:10; Gen. 3:15; Matt. 13:38, Isaiah 57:3-4). He has open contact; and he has a blood covenant with the spirit of error (Isaiah 28:15; 15:18).

Soothsayers, wizards, sorceresses, etc., are initiated into their practice by the blood of fowls, animals, and children (Isaiah 57:3-9). In like manner, the false prophet—the man—will be initiated into the mystery of lawlessness. As a result of this covenant by blood, the false **seer** now **possesses** the man, illegally. His visions from this dragon will be visions from hell (Isaiah 28:15, 18; Ezek. 13:6; Note: look up definitions).

The false prophet will set his **sight** (**vision**) to cause mankind to live under falsehood (i.e., the lie). He wants to brand as many as he can, destroying the rest (Isaiah 28:15; Rev. 13:15-18). The false prophet, the man, is bitterly zealous with this vision from the **earthy** spirit (James 3:15). This is because the spirit gave him a lying promise. The spirit in him lied to him by promising him **extended** life (Dan. 7:25). This truth will be developed in the final chapter.

In the last chapter, one will understand how the false prophet, along with the first beast, will try to prolong his days. I would also like to emphasize, at this point, that the spirit behind the man is the focus and thrust of this volume. It is necessary to warn the believers and the unbelieving of the reality of the operation of the dominion spirit, the false prophet. Why?

Hopefully, by the will of God the blind will see, in order that they don't fall into the pit following blind false prophets (Luke 6:39). With this in mind, I will now end this brief teaching on the man, the false prophet, and conclude this chapter with a second look at the emphasis of this book. This focus is the second beast, alias, **spirit** of error.

The spirit of error

1 John 4:1; 3; 6, KJV:
*¹ Beloved **believe not every spirit**, but try the spirits whether they are of God: because many false prophets are gone out into the world… ³And every **spirit** that confesseth not that Jesus Christ is come in the flesh is not of God: and this is that **spirit of antichrist**, whereof ye heard that it should come; and even **now** already is it in the world… ⁶We are of God, he that knoweth God, heareth us; he that is not of God, heareth not us. Hereby know we the **Spirit of truth**, and the **spirit of error**.*

John says believe not every **spirit**, because many false prophets are gone out into the world. So the false spirit is the one in the false prophets. He then called this spirit antichrist. Therefore, antichrist **is not** necessarily the first beast, **but the spirit that controls the false prophets.** This spirit dominates in the false prophets, because he is **the false prophet**. Luke bore witness to this truth in the book of Acts.

The spirit of python

Acts 16:16, KJV:
*And it came to pass, as we went to prayer, a certain damsel possessed with a spirit of **divination (lit., python)** met us, which brought her master much gain by **soothsaying***

Soothsaying is an Old English word that translates to "truth-saying." The damsel was saying the truth. Paul and his friends were **"servants of the Most High God."** But this insight was by an illegal prophet. Soothsaying is the Greek work manteuomai— to divine, to utter prophecy, oracle. It is from a root word mantis, which denotes a **seer, prophet, diviner.** So she saw by a seer, prophesied by this same prophet, and divined (determine) by this same diviner. She was soothsaying, because she was saying what the **seer** or prophet **in** her saw, and said. Do you see it?

Luke called this prophet in the woman "A **spirit of divination**" **(lit., "spirit python"),** which is a large serpent. Serpent is also the definition for **dragon** (Greek: drakon — a large serpent with keen power of sight). The serpent, or dragon, called python, will swallow you up, if he can mesmerize you with this **insight.** This is why God forbids mankind from seeking wizards, soothsayers, **physics**, etc.

They are actually seeking wisdom from snakes (Num. 24:1 — enchantment also means "serpents;" Gen. 3:1). The false prophet is among these serpents, or dragons, that see. His insight, though, is illegal, another definition for lawlessness. This makes him a pseudo (false) prophet. In Revelation 13 he is called "**another beast.**" In Revelation 16 he is called the "**false prophet.**"

Aliases

Rev. 16:13, KJV:
*And I saw three unclean spirits like frogs come out of the mouth of the dragon, come out of the mouth of the beast, and out of the mouth of the **false prophet.***

Rev. 19:20, KJV:
*And the beast was taken, and with him the **false prophet** that wrought miracles before him, with which he deceived them that had received the mark of the beast, and them what worshipped his image. These both were cast alive into a lake of fire burning with brimstone.*

Rev. 13:11, KJV:
*And I beheld **another beast** coming up out of the **earth;** and he had two horns like a lamb, and he spake as a dragon.*

The Scripture says it is the **false prophet** that worked miracles before the first beast. Revelation 13:11-12 says it is **another beast** who "… exerciseth all the power of the first beast before him."

"Another beast" is the false prophet in the spirit. He is also called the spirit of error, or the spirit of "plane" which denotes a planet **(earthly)** spirit. The Scripture teaches **God** shall permit the release of a **strong delusion,** in order that the hardhearted should believe a lie (2 Thess. 2:11). This verse literally reads, "And for this cause **God** shall send them **in-working of error** ("plane") that they should believe **the lie**." The in-working of "plane" (error) is supplied by the spirit of "plane" (error).

God shall allow a spirit of error, alias false prophet, to walk up out of the **earth**. He shall come out of the earth, because he is a **demonic earthly** spirit. In other words, his abode is on and under the earth. The false prophet is a beast who will manifest himself as the angels did in the days of Noah. He shall walk up out of the earth and deceive many. Those who are deceived shall **totally forsake** God, and marry **another** (2 Thess. 2:3).

Once again, the deceived shall spiritually marry the sons of God (Gen. 6). They shall **kiss** Satan and the first beast in marriage (Rev. 13:4). Mankind shall walk in **the lie, worshipping** the creature instead of the creator. It is this **lying worship** I will illustrate in the next chapter. It is a declaration from **above**. That is, the wisdom from above that God gives to those who ask (James 1:5; 3:17).

Chapter 5
The Spirit Giver

Rev. 13:15, KJV:
*And he had power to give **life (lit., spirit)** unto the image of the beast, that the image of the beast should both speak, and cause that as may as would not worship the image of the beast should be killed.*

There is an image of a beast that exists in every age that false prophets propagate. Yet in the age of the 8th beast, a "spirit" will be given to the beast image by the false prophet. The image of the 8the beast will be able to speak and take life. This image will also use death, in its many forms, to pressure humanity into worshipping the image of the beast. Image worship is worshipping a lie.

This is a lie of today—"image is everything." And whoever does not have this "image" that is supposedly "everything," they are killed by being looked down upon. This death comes through those who are already bearing the image of the beast. Or, some are being pressured to worship the worldly image of the beast. That is some are being pressured to become like the beast system of today, or else! Yet the image of the beast system of this present darkness is a lie.

The Father of Lies

The false prophet's message and purpose is "to give life" unto the image of the beast, which is **the lie** (Rev. 13:15). To give understanding concerning the lie, I will look first at the father of lies (John 8:44). In the beginning Jesus, who is truth, created Satan. He created him in truth, because "no lie is of *(lit., out of)* the truth" (1 John 2:21). Satan fathered lies himself. Lies did not come from God, because **"no lie is out of the truth."** The devil fathered the first lie.

Ezek. 28:14-15, KJV:
*[14]Thou are the anointed cherub that covereth; and I have set thee so: thou wast upon the holy mountain of God; thou hast walked up and down in the midst of the stones of fire. [15]Thou was **perfect (lit., complete, truth, integrity)** in thy ways from the day that thou was created, **till** iniquity was **found** in thee.*

John 8:44, KJV:
*Ye are of your father the devil, and the lust of your father ye will do. He was a **murderer (lit., manslayer)** from the beginning, **and abode not in the truth,** because there is no truth in him. When he speaketh a lie, he speaketh **of (Greek ek: out of)** his own: for he is **a liar** and the **father** of it.*

We see here that Satan is the father of lies. Lies did not exist until he fathered them. He fathered them for it is impossible for a lie to come out of God.[7] Satan was created in **truth and integrity.** But, something happened for him to father **lies.** He "abode not in the truth" (John 8:44). Ezekiel revealed he (Satan) was perfect in his ways **until** iniquity was found in him. How? He marketed himself. When he speaks of the lie, he speaks **out of himself.** He speaks out of himself, because he is selling himself.

Traveler or Wanderer?

Ezek. 28:16, KJV:
*By the multitudes of thy **merchandise (lit., travel, trade)** they have filled the midst of thee with **violence,** and thou has sinned: therefore I will cast thee as profane out of the mountain of God: and I will destroy thee, O covering Cherub, from the midst of the stones of fire.*

---

[7]*Note: God cannot lie. The devil cannot tell the truth (Dr. Turnel Nelson).*

It was Satan's "merchandise" (lit., travel, trade) that filled him with violence. Satan was a **traveler** before his fall; **and** he is still a traveler (Job 1:6-7). His travel corrupted him; because he, by comparison, saw how beautiful he was. In the words of Ezekiel, he (Satan) was perfect in **beauty**. He was the **king** of beautiful **stones** because, he was clothed with every **precious stones.** The workmanship of his tabrets (drums, cymbals) and **pipes** (lit., a bezel, carved out spot, for a **gem — a precious stone**) was prepared **in** him. (See Ezek. 28:13).

That is why he was king of Tyrus, meaning king of **stones.** Satan then began to merchandise himself and the stones of fire that he covered (Ezek. 28:16). This was done in the multitudes of his travels. In Satan's travels, he began to see how **beautiful** he was, compared to the other cherubs.

The other angels in turn saw his beauty, and many of the cherubs, with the abyss, set him on high (compare Ezek. 31:1-4). In his exaltation, he began to buy more worship by selling himself. "By the multitude of thy (Satan's) **merchandise**, they have filled the midst of thee (Satan) with violence" (Ezek. 28:16).

The end result of merchandising (buying and selling) is violence. He became so violent he slew **the man** (John 8:44). This is why false prophets are so violent against God's people. They are filled with the merchandising of the Satanic world (II Pet. 2:3, Mic. 3:5, Rev. 18:11-15). Merchandising - travel, buying, selling - became Satan's major work. He sold himself (John 8:44), and thus defiled his consecrated things (Ezek. 28:18).

In his travels, he fathered the first lie. He schemed himself as God; and thus sold himself as God. This is the lie. He says, "I am God, I sit in the seat of God" (Ezek. 28:2). He transformed himself **as** the light to make himself look like God (compare 2 Cor. 11:14). Thus some angels believed Satan was God. This is a great sin.

Satan was the first "who changed the truth of God into **a lie [lit; the lie]**" **(Rom. 1:25; John 8:44).**

The Lie-Homoerotic

Rom. 1:25, KJV:
*Who changed the truth of God into **a lie (lit., the lie)**, and **worshipped (lit., fear)** and served the creature more than the Creator, who is blessed for ever. Amen.*

This is the lie. It is when creature worship creature, instead of creature worshipping **creator. Jesus is the creator,** who is blessed forevermore. Satan caused angels to worship an angel. This kind of worship should not have happened. Thus, he fathered **the lie**, corrupting himself in it (Ezek. 28:17).

He and the angels who followed him, refused to retain God in their knowledge as the one to be worshipped (compare Rom. 1:28). Angel worshipping angel is the **same** as **men lying with men**. To God, angel worshipping angel, men worshipping men, or mankind worshipping angels, four footed beasts; birds, etc., are just like **homosexuals** (Rom. 1:25-28).

In the invisible realm, when the angels worshipped Satan, it was just like a **homosexual** act. Do you want to know where **homosexuality** came from? It came from Satan. He and the false prophet are **like homosexuals**. That is why most false prophets are sexually perverted (Jude; 2 Pet. 2:1-14; Num. 31:16 w/Num. 25). Therefore, homosexual comes from the words **homo** — same; and **sex** — one of the two divisions of human beings and animals. Hence, homosexuals are those who have sex with the same gender.

Satan, the false prophet, and all the angels that follow him, are homosexual. They are homosexuals, in the sense that they are worshipping each other—creatures of the **same gender**, or angels with angels. Worship is a form of intercourse, for the word worship means "to **kiss."** In the words of Paul, "they worshipped and served the creature more than the creator (Rom. 1:25).

They changed the truth (worshipping God) into **the lie** (worshipping each other). In other words, "they **changed** the glory of the incorruptible God into an image made like to corruptible man, and to birds, and four footed **beast**, and creeping things" (Rom. 1:23). This, O Friend of God is **the lie**; homosexuality.

In the days to come the angels who fell will literally be seen in the visible realm like the days of Noah (Gen. 6; Rev. 13). Mankind will once again have eye contact with these fallen angels. They will worship them, fulfilling the lie of homosexuality. The false prophet, alias another beast, is among these angels.

Cause and Effect

The false prophet and the dragon will come and use wonders of falsehood to **establish the final lie.** The dragon, that old serpent, who fathered the lie, will then **resurrect** the final lie. It is this lying wonder that will be discussed next. Then I will discuss the giver of life to the **image of the lie**, the false prophet himself.

In Revelation 12, the woman birthed a man-child. The dragon immediately tried to devour the **male** as soon as he (they) was born. However, the male child was seized to heaven; and as a result, the dragon was cast out of heaven into the earth (Rev. 12:4-8). The enraged dragon then proceeded to persecute the woman, because she was the one who birthed the male.

God, however, had ordained a **timely** deliverance for the woman. She was preserved in the **wilderness** from the face of the dragon. In his frustration "… the dragon was wroth with the woman, and went to make **war** on the **remnant** of her seed, which keep the command of God, and have the testimony of Jesus Christ" (Rev. 12:17). This woman and the man-child she birthed are the cause of Satan's warlike anger. The effect of this anger is the **rise** of the first beast.

Reanimation

Satan, alias dragon, now proceeded to use all his lawless power (2 Thess. 2:9, NIV). The mystery of iniquity will be unveiled (2 Thess. 2:8). Iniquity is defined as lawlessness, without law, or **illegality** (Strong's #458). Therefore, it is illegal for Satan to do what he is about to do. He stood upon the sand of the sea and **resurrected** the **beast.**

Rev. 12:17-18, The Worrel New Testament:
17And the dragon was angry with the woman, and went away to make war with the rest of her seed, who keep the commandments of God, and have the testimony of Jesus; 18and he stood upon the sand of the sea.

Rev. 13:1, The Worrel New Testament:
And I saw a beast coming up out of the sea, having ten horns and seven heads, and on his horns ten diadems, and upon his heads names of blasphemy.

In Revelation 13:1, the King James says, "And **I** stood upon the sand of the sea," as if to say, John stood on the sea. However, in one of the oldest text, as seen in Worrel's Translation, it literally reads, "And **he** [the dragon, Rev. 12:17] stood upon the sand of the sea" (Rev. 12:18). The New International Version (NIV) says, "And the **dragon** stood on the shore of the sea" (Rev. 13:1).

Finally, the New American Bible says, "**It** took its position on the sand of the sea" (Rev. 12:18).

This is significant because **"it"**[8] is the dragon, not John, who empowers the beast up from the sea and abyss (2 Thess. 2:9, NIV). Thus, the **final lie** is going to be manifested through the works of lawlessness. In Chapter One, I reviewed some works of the mystery of lawlessness. Now let us see some of its aspects.

Remember, the false prophets **thought** they were doing mighty **works** in the name of Jesus. When, in fact, they were doing their deeds by the **works** of **lawlessness** (see Chapter 1 exposition of Matt. 7:22-23). It is by this work of Satan's power the beast will be resurrected. The beast looks like a leopard (a four footed beast; Rom. 1:23, 25).

Rev. 13:2-3, KJV:
*²And the beast which I saw was like unto a **leopard**, and his feet were as the feet of a bear, and his mouth as the mouth of a lion: and the dragon gave him his power, and his seat, and great authority. ³And I saw one of his heads as it were **wounded to death (lit., stroke of death)**; and his deadly wound was healed: and all the world wondered after the beast.*

The world wondered after the beast, because his stroke of death was **healed.** In other words, one of his "heads" was dead. Yet, it is resurrected by the **power** of Satan (2 Thess. 2:9, 11). The beast had a "wound by a sword and **did live**" (Rev. 13:14). Hear what the angel says to John in Rev. 17:8, "The beast that thou sawest **was** (he existed before), and **is not** (he died); and shall ascend (lit., walk up) out of the bottomless pit (he lives again), and shall go

---

[8] *Note: If one was to use the Received Text or the Majority Texts that reads as the King James translation "And I [John] stood ...." In lieu of "... the dragon stood," the dragon is still the catalyst be which the beast arose, as seen in context of Revelation 12:17; Revelation 13:2, etc.*

into perdition: **And** they that dwell on the earth shall **wonder**..."
Why?

Because they **beheld** the beast that was (lived once already), and is not (the beast died before), and **yet is** — he lives again (Rev. 17:8). In the mind of these people, they are stunned at the fact that this beast was dead. "**Yet**" he is **living** again. This act of the beast living again...is...**a false resurrection**; a lying wonder, or a **wonder of falsehood** (2 Thess. 2:9).

Mystery of Iniquity Revitalized

The mystery of **iniquity (lit., lawlessness)** is already working. The restrainer (falling away) must come first, then "shall that **wicked (lit., lawless one)** be revealed" (2 Thess. 2:8). He will be revealed out of the sea of humanity, and out of the bottomless pit. This is why those, whose names are not written in the Lamb's Book of Life, **wondered** at the beast (Rev. 17:8). The world wondered because Satan did something **forbidden**, concerning the abyss, which will be discussed in volume two.

Rev. 17:9-11, KJV:
*⁹And here is the mind which hath wisdom. The seven heads are seven mountains, on which the **woman** sitteth. ¹⁰And there are seven kings: five are fallen, and one is, and the other is not yet come; and when he cometh, he must continue a short space. ¹¹And the beast that **was**, and **is not**, even he is the eighth, and is **of (lit., out of)** the seven, and goeth into perdition.*

In Rev. 17:9 John says the **heads** of the beast are kings. Revelation 13 says one of the beast's heads received a **stroke** of death by a sword, but **did live** (Rev. 13:12, 14). It is this head (king), who once died by the sword, but in that day he will live by the **power of lawlessness.** The angel says, the eighth beast came "out of the seven" **that existed before.** Listen to the angel again.

Rev. 17:10, KJV:
*And there are seven kings: **five are fallen**, and **one** is, and **the other is not yet come**; and when he cometh, he must continue a short space.*

The numbers of kings total seven. It is **out of** these seven the eighth beast will be resurrected. "And the beast that **was** and **is not**, even he is the **eighth**, and is of **(lit., out of)** the seven, and goeth into perdition" (Rev. 17:11). Do you see it? He is called the eight, because eight means **new beginning.** "Eighth" also denotes that he will have all the resurrected characteristics of the seven kings that ruled. However, don't forget, the eighth **lived before** as one of the seven. The scripture says, Satan will work "all power," not, some power (2 Thess. 2:9). What is "all power?"

"All power" can include the resurrection from the dead. It is the ultimate wonder of **falsehood** that Satan will perform. The false prophet will reinforce it by making a **inanimate** image **live**. Remember, Jesus says, "And many false prophets shall **rise**, and shall **deceive many**" (Matt. 24:11). The word rise also means to **resurrect** (Matt. 27:63; Mk. 12:26).

There shall be false resurrections done by false prophets. The false prophet will give **spirit** to the **image of the lie**, causing this dumb idol to **rise**. First, Satan initiated the lie by causing worship to himself. Then he resurrected a beast, which caused the people to **walk** in the lie by worshipping the beast. Next, his personal prophet, alias another beast, shall give life to the **image** of the lie, raising it also. Sadly, some shall worship the image also!

Self Worship

Rev. 13:11-14, KJV:
*[11] And I beheld another beast **coming up out of the earth;** and he had two horns like a lamb, and he spake as a dragon. [12]And he exerciseth **all the power** of the first beast before him, and causeth the earth and them*

which dwell therein to worship the first beast, whose deadly wound was healed. ¹³And he doeth great wonders, so that he maketh fire come down from heaven on the earth in the sight of men, ¹⁴And deceiveth them that dwell on the earth by the means of those miracles which he had power to do in the sight of the beast; saying to them that dwell on the earth, that they should make an image to the beast, which had the wound by a sword, and did live

Before we continue on with the rest of the verses, let us take a look at some key words in what is already stated. One of the first things one can see is that the false prophet, by **influence,** controlled the people who were deceived. This was done by the miracles he did.

The deception is for them to make an image **"to"** the beast, not just **"of"** the beast, but also **"to"** the beast. This is significant. Because, this arrogant king (the beast) will not worship anything, but **himself!**

Dan. 11:36-37, KJV:
*³⁶And the king shall do according to his will; and he shall **exalt himself, and magnify himself** above every god, and shall speak marvelous things against the God of gods and shall prosper till the indignation be accomplished: for that that is determined shall be done. ³⁷Neither shall he regard the God of his fathers, **nor desire women,** nor **regard** any god: for he shall magnify **himself above all.***

From these verses we can see that the beast won't **tolerate** the worshipping of any other gods. He also does not desire women (homoerotic). In the words of Paul, "He opposeth and exalteth himself above **all** that is **called** God or that is worshipped" (2 Thess. 2:4).

Therefore, the only **image** he would accept is an image **to** him. This is because he only **"acknowledges"** himself. He worshipped himself over God, and the people worshipped the creature (the beast) over the creator.

Thus shall he [the beast] do "in the ... strongholds" (his own "imaginations" (Dan 11:39 w/2 Cor 10:4-5)) with a strange (different) god whom **he** shall acknowledge (Dan. 11:39). I repeat again, which to me indeed is not burdensome, but for you it is safe (Phil. 3:1).

The only god whom the beast acknowledges is the image god of **himself.** Little children, keep yourselves from idols [lit., **image** (i.e., for worship)]. Image worship is **self**-centered (See I John 5:21). Image worship is a preparation to accept him who worships **himself.**

Wrong Photocopy

There is another aspect of this image **to** the beast: Mankind will become the image of the beast, as Christ is the **image** of the invisible God (Col. 1:15). Jesus is the express image of God's person (Heb. 1:3). The words **"express image"** literally denote **"charakter."** We get our English word characteristics from this word. The word **"mark"** used for the mark of the beast is the Greek word **charagma (**akin to the Greek **charakter).** This tells us that the **mark** of the beast is the **characteristic** of the beast, as you will see shortly.

However, all that Christ exemplified in his life and death were the character of God. God's characteristics are love, long-suffering, mercy, goodness, patience, etc. (see Ex. 34:6-7). Jesus Christ expressed these characteristics perfectly when He was in the flesh. Therefore, He is the image of God. When a person saw Jesus, he/she saw **God.** Hallelujah!

The people who were deceived by the false prophet, on the other hand, made an image **to** the beast (Rev. 13:14). This word **image** in Revelation is a Greek word, which demonstrates the same meaning in two different realms. The Greek word for image is "eikon," meaning likeness. Our English word icon is derived from eikon. An icon is usually a picture or image of a person. Jesus is "the **image** of the invisible God" (Col. 1:15).

The deceived made "an **image** to the beast." Therefore, when the people made an image **to** the beast, they in essence, took on his character. Their lifestyle was to the beast. That is, they pleased him, instead of God. What a tragedy to become beastly, when man was created in the **image of God**. Mankind has lowered itself to take on the image of a leopard beast.

This leopard had a name. The word "name" can be defined as authority, nature or character. His name is blasphemy (Rev. 13:1), and that is what he did, blaspheme God. The beast's name, **blas<u>phemy</u>** ("phemy," transliterated into English as "fame"), literally means — **to hinder fame, or to speak evil against fame.** What fame? In this setting the beast spoke against the **fame of God**.

Fame

Luke 4:14, KJV:
*And Jesus returned in the **power of the Spirit** into Galilee: and there went out a **fame** of him throughout all the region round about.*

Luke says, the **fame** of Jesus was by the **power of the spirit**. The scribes, however, said He did it by an **unclean spirit. This is <u>blasphemy,</u> calling the power of the spirit the work of an unclean spirit.**

Mark 3:28-30, KJV:
*²⁸Verily I say unto you, all sins shall be forgiven unto the sons of men, and blasphemies wherewith soever they shall blaspheme. ²⁹But he that **blaspheme against the Holy Ghost** hath never forgiveness, but is in danger (lit., **hold in guilt**) of eternal damnation: ³⁰**Because they said, He hath an unclean spirit.***

As one can see, even the Pharisees of that day were walking in the **name** of the beast, which is blasphemy. Likewise the people made an image to the beast by taking on his characteristics. Let us see an example.

Rev. 16:8-9; KJV:
*⁸And the fourth angel poured out his vial upon the **sun**; and power was given unto him to scorch men with fire. ⁹ And **men** were scorched with great heat, and **blasphemed** the **name of God**, which hath power over these plagues: and they repented not to give him glory.*

Rev. 16:21, KJV:
*And there fell upon men a great hail out of heaven, every stone about the weight of a talent: and men **blasphemed** God because of the plague of the hail; for the plague thereof was exceeding great.*

Mankind, during the times of judgment, took on the image of the beast. This is demonstrated in the fact of what came out of their mouths -**blasphemy**. Thus, the name of the beast can also be in the mouth (Jude 14-15).

The Dumb Idol That Spoke

Once the image of the beast was made, literally, "with men's hands" (Acts. 17:22-25; Rev. 13:17), and spiritually within men's heart, then the false prophet gave **"life"** unto this detestable abomination.

Rev. 13:15, KJV:
*And he had power to give **life (lit., spirit)** unto the **image** of the beast, **that** the image of the beast should **both speak**, and cause that as many as should not worship the image of the beast should be killed.*

In the generations, past and present, mankind worshipped dumb idols (images). Those images could not talk, see, hear nor walk. But when the lawless powers of Satan manifest themselves, in the latter days, angels shall give **spirit** to the idols of the earth. Paul says when a person worships idols, he is actually worshipping the demon (spirit) behind the idols (1 Cor. 10:19-21). But in these days, men will be worshipping an image possessed by a spirit. It will be able to speak and kill by words. An unclean spirit, giving it life, will possess the image of Revelation 13.

The false prophet will copy God's work in Genesis 2:7. Genesis teaches that God breathed into man and he became a living soul. Likewise, the false prophet shall cause an unclean spirit to come out of his mouth and enter into the image to the beast, giving it **life**. This will be another one of his false miracles. Let's hear what John saw. "And I saw **three unclean spirits** like frogs come out of the mouth of the dragon, and out of the mouth of the beast, and **out of the mouth** of the **false** prophet" (Rev. 16:13).

Where did these spirits go, and what are they for? They are for the **spirit** of **devils** working **miracles.** (Rev. 16:14). In the case of the false prophet, his miracle is when the spirit left his mouth it entered into the **image** and made it **live** (Rev. 13:13-15). Remember, the false prophet deceives by miracles (Rev. 13:13-15, Rev. 16:14). Now, we can understand more clearly the words of our Lord Jesus.

Matt. 24:24, KJV:
*For there shall arise **false Christs**, and **false prophets**, and shall **shew** great signs and wonders; insomuch that, if it were **possible (lit., able, capable)** they shall deceive the very elect.*

The false prophet will show so many miracles people will say, "He must be real." Thus, they shall fall away from God. If he is **"able"** to, and he is **"capable,"** he....**can**....deceive. The Lord warned the children of Israel of the same thing.

Deut. 13:1-3, KJV:
*¹ If there arise among you a prophet, or a dreamer of dreams, any **giveth** thee a sign or a **wonder**, ²And the sign and the wonder come to pass, whereof he spake unto thee, saying, let us go after other gods which thou has **not known**, and let us serve them; ³Thou shall **not** hearken unto the words of that prophet, or that dreamer of dreams: for the Lord your God **proveth** you, to know whether ye **love** the lord your God with all your heart and with all your soul.*

One should compare these verses above with Rev. 13:11-13. This is going to be the test of the Church in the twelve hundred and sixty days of pressure. The Church must keep the **commandments** of **God,** and the **faith of Jesus** (Rev. 14:12). None in the Church should fall away from God, and receive "the mark of [the beast's] name" (Rev. 14:11).

Marked to Perdition (666)

The miracle of the false prophet will be so potent that he will cause all (those who will be deceived) to receive the mark of the beast name, or "the number of his name." It is only those who have the wisdom of God from above who will be able to know the number of the beast, and deny it.

Rev. 13:18, KJV:
Here is wisdom. Let him that hath understanding **count** *(lit., a stone used for voting) the number of the beast: for it is the number of a man (lit; because of man); and his number is Six hundred threescore and six.*

This is one of the reasons why God has released me to speak **to** the purpose of the false prophet. Jesus Christ wants His Church to know **an aspect** of the "count" of the beast that you may stand the test of the time to come. In the time to come, the false prophet will promulgate (spread) the mark of the beast. First, he will deceive the people by influence, to "make an image to the beast," by copying his character. Then he, along with the **speaking image**, will use unmerciful force to make the people receive the beast's mark. This mark of the beast exists in many forms. **There is a literal mark; and there is a mark in nature or "character."**

There is the *mark* of the beast, the *name* of the beast, and the *number* of his name. Revelation 14:11 call it the *mark of his name*. In Revelation 16:2, the writer calls it the *mark of the beast*. These are all important synonyms. They give clearer understanding concerning the "count" of the beast.

The Scripture uses words like mark, and name of the beast, and number of his name (Rev. 13:17). The "mark" is the **"mark of his name"** (Rev. 14:11). The "number" is **"the number of his name"** (Rev. 13:17); and the mark of the beast (Rev. 16:2) is the **"name of the beast"** (Rev. 13:17). The common denominator in all these synonyms is "name." What is the beast's name? His name is blasphemy (Rev. 13:1).

Blasphemy is man's arrogance against God. Thus, the number 666 is the "count" of a man. The **count (or vote)** of his name denotes man's blasphemy or arrogance against God. This is exemplified in Goliath—the Giant **beastly** seed of the fallen angels—in conflict with David, Jesus, in type. Goliath's **height** (lit., arrogance, Strong's #1363) was **six** cubits and a span (the spread of the fingers). Thus, Goliath's **"arrogance"** was **"six"** cubits, **and** "the spread of the finger."

Remember, Adam was also created on the **sixth** day. Thus, six is the number that is **voted** as man's count. This compliments the book of Revelation beautifully; because the number "of a **man"** is **six-six-six (666).** The name of the beast is blasphemy, which is man's **arrogance** (Rev. 13:1 with 13: 6). Thus, the name of his number; or the mark of his name; or the name of the beast is man's arrogance against Jesus; even as Goliath was arrogant against David and his God.

1 Sam. 17:45, KJV:
*Then said David to the Philistine, thou comest to me with a sword, and with a spear, and with a shield: but I come to thee in the name of the Lord of hosts, the God of the armies of Israel, whom thou has **defied** (lit., pull off, strip, defame).*

It was in the **forehead** of Goliath that David threw the stone that killed him (see 1 Sam. 17:49). His **mind** was full of **defamation.** So it is on the **forehead or mind** of the people, which shall be branded. The deceived shall receive the "count" of his mark. It will be physical; but for sure, it will be in man's character first (Rev. 16:10-11; Rev. 16:21; Rev. 17:3).

Mankind in their minds, hands, and mouth will become arrogant against God. They will receive the number of his name, and will not relent in **speaking against** the God of gods. As a result, God's anger will be kindled against this prophet that causes mankind to err. God shall deal with him in the time of his visitation. The Lord shall not show mercy.

Rom. 12:1-2, KJV:
¹beseech you therefore brethren by the mercies of God, that you present your bodies a living sacrifice, holy acceptable unto God, which is your

*reasonable service. ²And be **not** conformed to this world: **but** be ye transformed by the renewing of your **mind**, that ye may prove what is that good, and acceptable, and perfect will of God.*

May the Lord Jesus Christ bless you, and keep you from the pollution of the idol(s), present or future. The Lord God shall pour out his indignation upon the angels behind the idols. In fact, he created a special place for these angels, **the lake of fire.** It is in this **second death** the false prophet shall be cast down and meet his **demise.**

Chapter 6
The False Prophet's Demise

Rev. 19:20, KJV:
*And the beast was taken, and with him the **false prophet** that wrought miracles before him, with which he deceived them that had received the mark of the beast, and them that worshipped his image. **These both** were cast **alive** into a lake of fire burning with brimstone.*

The Holy Spirit directed me to expose the purpose of the false prophet. He also instructed me to cast him down, and speak of the false prophet's demise. **Demise** means a transfer of royal power by **death** or abdication. Therefore, I conclude this volume with the extinction of the false prophet. To do this, let us begin our study in the book of Daniel.

Daniel wrote of how King Nebuchadnezzar received from God, a dream (Dan. 2:28). In the king's vision, he saw the splendor of **four** kingdoms. In other visions, Daniel, a prophet, saw these same beautiful kingdoms of gold, silver, brass, iron and clay as **beasts.** But the king did not remember or know the interpretation of the dream.

However, after Daniel prayed to God, he received the revelation of this mysterious dream in a night vision (Dan. 2:19). It was after the unveiling of the mystery that Daniel worshipped God **in** what he saw. Nebuchadnezzar saw a "great image" of **different** materials. But Daniel, by the vision, understood the different materials to be the **rise** and **fall** of kingdoms. Daniel also understood that God, the Father is the one who allow kings to rule; and it is also God, the Father who also deposes kings according to His will.

Sovereign Lord

Dan. 2:20-21, KJV:
[20]Daniel answered and said, Blessed be the name of God for ever and ever: for wisdom and might are his: *[21]And he* **changeth the times** *and the seasons:* **he removeth kings** *and setteth up kings: he giveth wisdom unto the wise, and knowledge to them that know understanding*

In these verses, Daniel declared that **God** changes (lit., alter) **times** and seasons. He "**removeth** kings and setteth up kings" (Dan.2:21). This is a **key** to understand the length of times and seasons angels rule in the **invisible**. Paul says, "The **invisible** things of him are clearly seen being **understood** by the things that are made" (Rom 1:20). It is God who **sets up** and **removes** kings in the visible, as well as in the **invisible**. We understand this by what "visible" history tells us, concerning changes in world powers.

Set Time (42 Months)

Nothing is changed, or established except by the **word of God.** It is God who gives ruling angels their allotted **time** over the nations they rule. Angels, authorities, and powers are **subjected** to Jesus (I Pet. 3:22). The first beast and the false prophet are also **subjected** to a time. However, they, knowing their time span is short, shall set their heart to **alter** the **time** of God.

Dan 7:25, KJV:
And he shall speak great words against the most High, and shall **wear out (lit., wear out mentally)** *the saints of the most High, and* **think to change (lit., alter)** *times and* **laws (lit., royal edicts):** *and they shall be given into his hand* **until** *a time, times, and the dividing of time.*

I included the false prophet; because he exercises all the **power (lit., authority)** of the first beast before him (Rev. 13:12). One might ask, what authority of the first beast? The authority to cause false miracles is part of this false license. But there is more.

Rev. 13:5, KJV:
And there was given unto him a mouth speaking great things and blasphemies; and **power (lit., authority)** *was given unto him* **to continue (lit; make or do)** *forty and two* **months.**

The first beast was given authority **"to make"** (i.e., live, or also **"to make war"**[9]) time, times, and dividing of a time, which is 42 months (Rev. 13:5). This is the **lawless authority** given by Satan to the beast (Rev. 13:2). Yet there is a paradox, God allowed it (2 Thess. 2:9; 2:11).

This authority was given because **power** cannot work without authority, even though it is lawless (contrast Luke 10:19; Rev. 9). Satan, by his **"all power"** (2 Thess. 2:9), caused the beast to live again. However, for this lawless resurrection to **work**, authority had to be given unto him.

This is why the **beast** was given "power" and **"great authority"** (Rev. 13:2). It's **great**, because the beast was resurrected and allowed **"to do" (make war or live) for** 42 months. However, it is the false prophet who will exercise all this authority.

He, along with the beast, will work hand in hand, **attempting** to alter the time God ordained for them. They shall **"hope"** to change times and laws. The false prophet will **attempt** to keep the beast alive beyond the forty-two months.

Thus, the beast **foolishly** makes war with Him who controls time (Rev. 17:14; Dan. 7:25; 8:25). This "head" that had the stroke of

---

[9]*As stated in the Majority Texts (Byzantine Texts)*

death, yet lived, shall **try** to defy God's time. Why? This is because they know their demise **must** come (Rev. 12:12). "For at the **time appointed** the end shall be" (Dan. 8: 19b).

The beast to come, and the false prophet, knows they will be the **first** to go to into the lake of fire. So they will try, frantically, to change times set for them. Satan himself had to be **"laid hold on"** that the angel might **bind** him for a time of one thousand years in the **torment** of the **abyss** (Rev. 20:1-3; Ezek. 31:11-15).

The words **"laid hold on,"** literally means **"to use strength."** The angel had to use strength because the encounter was a wrestling. Nobody wants to burn, no! Not even the angels for whom the lake of fire was prepared (Matt. 25:41). Furthermore, to solidify the truth that angels do resist their demise, let's look, again, in the book of the "greatly beloved" Daniel.

Rulers of Darkness Bound to God's Time

Dan. 10:11-13, KJV:
*11And he said unto me, O Daniel, a man greatly beloved, understand the words that I speak unto thee, and stand upright: for unto thee am I now sent. And when he had spoken this word unto me, I stood trembling. 12Then said he unto me, Fear not, Daniel: for from the first day that thou didst set thine heart to understand, and to chasten thyself before thy God, thy words were heard, and I am come for thy words. 13But the prince of the kingdom of Persia **withstood** me one and twenty days: but, lo, Michael, one of the chief princes, came to help me; **and I remained there with the kings of Persia.***

Daniel was seeking understanding from God. The first day he called upon God, he was heard. He was seeking understanding concerning the next kingdom to arise. So God sent the angel Gabriel9 with the answer. The prince of Persia, however, held up Gabriel, for twenty-one days. It is from this encounter, we will learn that angels do **attempt** to **alter** "set seasons" of God. At the end of Daniel's twenty-one day fast, Gabriel got through to Daniel.

Dan. 10:20-21, KJV:
*20Then said he, Knowest thou wherefore I come unto thee? and now will I **return to fight** with the **prince of Persia:** and when I am gone forth, lo, the **prince of Grecia** shall come. 21But I will shew thee that which is noted in the scripture of truth: and there is none that **holdeth** with me in **these** things, but Michael your prince.*

Dan. 11:1, KJV:
*Also I in the **first** year of Darius the Mede, even I, stood to confirm and to strengthen him.*

One must know that God will declare in the earth what is already written in heaven. God revealed to Daniel what was "noted in the scripture of truths" in heaven. These particular truths were concerning the rise and fall of kings in the earth. However, the princes of darkness knew this, and **tried** to delay their **demise**.

This is because, once that which is written in heaven is revealed **under** heaven, especially to God's prophets, it is under the **law of time** (**Ecclesiastes. 3:1**; Amos 3:7; **Rev. 10:7**). Therefore, no fallen angel can alter God's set time under heaven. Yet in vain they try.

In this case, Gabriel encountered the prince (or principality) of Persia, who was **withstanding** the change of God. God had ordained another angel, the **prince of Greece**, to be the next ruler. In the words of Gabriel, "the prince of Grecia shall **come**" (Dan. 10:20). Going contrary, the angelic prince of Persia had "**hoped**" to "**alter**" God's set time. He blatantly "withstood" Gabriel (Dan. 10:13).

The struggle became so fierce that Michael, one of the chief princes, had to come and help Gabriel. The understanding is this:

the time for each prince's rule is already established and written in the heavens (Dan. 10:21; Rev. 20:1-3). The angel says, "But I will shew thee that which is noted in the scripture of truth" (Dan. 10:21).

This particular truth is that the **rule** of Persia is close to ending. The prince/king of Grecia must now begin to rule. Gabriel continued saying, "and there is none that **holdeth (lit., bind; compare Rev. 20:2)** with me in these things, but Michael your prince." Michael had to help Gabriel **bind** the prince of Persia to his allotted **time (compare Rev. 20:3)**. This was not the first encounter Michael and Gabriel had with fallen angels, who resisted the end of their domination.

When Babylon's time was at hand, **king Heylel** resisted Michael, who was trying to **bind** him that the **spirit** of Mede might rule. Let's look at the Scripture again. "Also I [Gabriel] in the first year of Darius the Mede [the time when Darius conquered Babylon[10]; even I [Gabriel], stood to confirm and to strengthen him [Michael]." How do I know it was Michael?

The answer is that Daniel 11:1 is a continuation of Daniel 10:21, and at the end of Daniel 10:21 Gabriel's **subject** was his fellow archangel **Michael.** So Gabriel had to come and "strengthen" Michael, the archangel, that they together might **"bind"** king Heylel (Isaiah 14:12), the principality of Babylon, to God's **time**; because at the close of that era, it was **time** for "the **spirit** of the kings of the Medes" to rule (Jer. 51:11; Isaiah14).

God's Royal Edict - It's Law

These fallen angels were trying to hinder the **book of truth** from being fulfilled, then, and now. But Gabriel declared it anyway.

---

[10]See Dan. 5:30-31; Dan. 9:1

God's declaration is law and no man, angel or beast, can stop the Word of His power. The ages were framed by the Word of God (Heb. 11:3). He upholds, and destroys by the Word of His power (Heb. 1:3; II Pet. 3:5-7). Our God is the Strongest of the strong (1 Cor. 1:25). **His truth** of the appointed times stands.

Dan. 11:2-3, KJV:
²And now I will shew thee the **truth.** *Behold there shall stand up yet* **three kings** *in Persia; and the fourth shall be far richer than all: and by his strength through his riches he shall stir up all against the* **realm of Grecia.** *³And a mighty king shall stand up, that will rule with* **great** *dominion, and do according to his will.*

So likewise, it is "noted in the scripture of truth" (the Bible) that the first beast shall only **"make"** forty-two months. Yet the beast, Satan, and the false prophet shall try to hinder the truth of what is written. They shall **"hope"** to change **times** (42 months) and **laws (lit., royal edicts)** (Dan. 7:25).

However, **rest in God**, for the strong angels are standing together with God to ensure the word of God is fulfilled (Rev. 201-3; Dan. 10:13 & 21; Rev. 5:2; Rev. 18:1). For it is God who removes kings and sets up both natural and (see Dan. 2:21). The false prophet's removal shall come. He shall be **"taken" (arrested: Strong's #4084)** and **cast** down into the sea of fire (Rev. 19:20). It is with this understanding of his **demise** that this volume will be concluded.

God's Region of Fire

In the book of Ezekiel 22:31, God declared that He would judge the false prophets. This judgment is by fire. They have "burned" the saints. They shall also burn. In the words of the Lord, "**their own way** have I recompensed upon their heads" (Ezek. 22:31).

Ezek. 22:31, KJV:
*Therefore have I poured out mine indignation upon them; I have consumed them with the **fire of my wrath:** their own way have I recompensed upon their heads, saith the Lord God.*

The middle part of this verse literally reads, "I have consumed them with the **fire of my region across.**" The word **wrath** is the feminine (receiver) for the word that means **region across** or the opposite side (Strong's #5678, #5676). Therefore, the Spirit of God is actually saying that the **false prophets** will be consumed with the **fire across the region**—the "region" of the lake of fire. It is in this **region** the false prophet shall meet **death by fire.**

Death by Fire

First, Jesus Christ shall **descend** during the time of **the** battle (Ezek. 13:5; Rev. 16:14-15). In this battle the kingdoms of this world shall become the kingdoms of our **Lord** and **his Christ.** He shall reign forever and ever, meaning the power of the kingdoms (Matt. 4:8-9) will be Christ's (Rev. 11:15; Eph. 1; Rev. 10:7). **Jesus Christ and His Church** shall **take power and dominion** from the dragon, the beast and the false prophet (Dan. 7:26). This is the beginning of the false prophet's demise.

Daniel 7:26, KJV:
*But the judgment shall sit, and they shall **take away (or destroy)** his dominion, to consume and to destroy [it] unto the end.*

Do you see it? Jesus and His Church (the judgment) shall take away all the dominion of the fourth kingdom. The false prophet, who used the authority of the beast, and the power of miracles, shall **lose his power**. The false prophet will be among the first angels to die the "second death" in the lake of fire. But! I thought spirits couldn't die? Look again; and **death,** a spirit being; and **hell (the whole underworld herself)** were cast into the lake of fire. **This "lake of fire" is "the second death"** (Rev. 20:14). The lake of fire is the **ultimate** death. It is in this second death all the angels who transgressed shall meet their demise. God shall strip them of their royal powers by abdication; and He shall cast them into the "second death" or "lake of fire" (Rev. 20:14).

Rev. 19:20, KJV:
*And the beast was **taken**, and with him the **false prophet** that wrought miracles before him with which he deceived them that had received the mark of the beast, and them that worshipped his image. **These both** were cast **alive** into a lake of fire, burning with brimstone.*

He that hath an ear let him hear what the Spirit says to the Churches. There is coming a time when a vast majority of mankind shall totally fall away from God. The dominion from the unseen shall manifest himself clearly to deceive. This dominion prophet shall do great signs and wonders, deceiving the world. He shall also try to prolong his days; but God shall bring him to a **"full stop."**

The false prophet shall be stopped in the lake of fire. The controller, who once controlled the deceived, shall himself be dominated forever, and ever, and ever.... In the royal edict, it is **written**, "And the devil that deceived them, was cast into the lake of fire and brimstone, where the beast and the false prophet **are,** and shall be **tormented day and night** forever and ever"(Rev. 20:10).

In conclusion, may the Lord Jesus Christ strengthen you, the believer, to stand in the day of battle, as we (the Church) brace ourselves for continued martyrdom! I pray this volume has worked in you the faith of Jesus—the faith to resist the false prophet's spirit, who is already working in his prophets; the faith to die for Jesus rather than take the mark (character) of the beast. Brothers, and sisters, I pray the grace of our Lord Jesus Christ be with you, and towards you. Amen!

Notes

Notes

Notes

Notes

Other Books

Poiema, by Judith Peart: A collection of poetry written by Judith Peart; and illustrations by one of her sons Jeshua David Peart

Wisdom From Above, by Judith Peart: A biblically based booklet of quotes for practical living.

Sexual Healing, by Judith Peart, FOREWORD: "Your hearts will be touched, your feelings, and emotions challenged as you read this book … Thank you Judith for your courage and transparency to help others as the Holy Spirit has helped you. Freely you have received. Freely you have given" (Dr. Sandra Phillips Hayden).

100 Never, by Judith Peart: Quotes to Help Women Improve Their Marriage Relationship

The Lamb, by Donald Peart: This book is a detailed look at the Lamb of God. He is King and Lord. We explore His wonderful character and work as it relates to our expected lifestyle, self-esteem and relational living. The book starts with His blood that "speaks better things."

Jesus' Resurrection, Our Inheritance, by Donald Peart: This book is a detailed look at the resurrection of Jesus Christ and the two phases associated with each of the four resurrections.

Sex Pleasures, By Donald Peart: This book is a detailed look at some of the vices of sexuality (apparent pleasures) that have damaged many, with the view to bring healing through the forgiveness of Jesus.

Forgiven 490, by Donald Peart w/Judith Peart: Jesus said "every sin and blasphemy shall be forgiven unto men," except for one particular blasphemy. Jesus wants to deliver all of mankind by forgiving us, and teaching us how to forgive others!

The Days of the Seventh Angel, By Donald Peart: A volume of the eschatology series that opens the mystery of God relative to the seventh angel who sounds the last trumpet.

The Torah (The Principle) of Giving, by Donald Peart: The text is a guide for those who desire to be a giver in the right way. It will release the bound from the curse of the law. Yet, the book will help the reader develop responsible giving.

The Time Came, by Donald Peart: The appearing of Jesus, in person, 2,000 years ago was the sign that that age was effectively over. The change of these ages *"into the age"* to come is also in a Person—*"the Lord's Christ,"* both head and body. Jesus **is** *"the beginning **and the end.**"*

The Last Hour, The First Hour, The Forty-Second Generation, by Donald Peart: This book explores the book of Revelations, the book of Daniel, the Gospels, and so on to unveil an understanding of times

Vision Real, by Donald Peart: What is real vision? Is vision animate or a real person?

The False Prophet, Alias, Another Beast V1, by Donald Peart is a comprehensive study manual that exposes "another beast," and his purpose.

"the beast" V2, by Donald Peart: "Then the angel said to me: " 'Why are you astonished? I will explain to you the mystery of …the beast….'"

Son of Man Prophesy Against the false prophet …," V2.1, by Donald Peart: This volume is a comprehensive instruction booklet that prophesies **against** "the false prophet," which is the spirit of Antichrist.

The Dragon's Tail (The Many False Prophets), V3, by Donald Peart: The seven headed dragon in the book of Revelation used his tail to fling. His seven heads are seven ruling angels—who dominate some so-called "elders…" His "tail" is a metaphor for the "many false prophets."

The Work of Lawlessness Revealed, by Donald Peart: a detailed look at the 2 Thessalonians 2, discussing topic like mystery of lawlessness, the man of sin who acts like God in the temple of God, etc.

When God Made Satan, by Donald Peart: a book that discusses the origin of Satan as opposed to Mr. and Mrs. Adam.

CROWN OF GLORY MINISTRIES
P.O. Box 1041 Randallstown, MD 21133
E-mail: secretary@crownofgloryministries.net
Secretary Phone: 410-905-0308

www.ingramcontent.com/pod-product-compliance
Lightning Source LLC
Chambersburg PA
CBHW031203090426
42736CB00009B/768